This is
THE PHILIPPINES

This is
THE PHILIPPINES

Text and photographs by Nigel Hicks

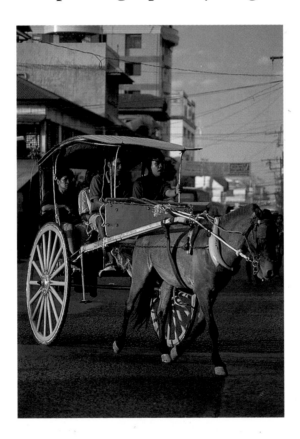

NEW HOLLAND

This edition published in 2001 by
New Holland Publishers (UK) Ltd
London • Cape Town • Sydney • Auckland

www.newhollandpublishers.co.uk

86-88 Edgware Road
London W2 2EA, United Kingdom

80 McKenzie Street
Cape Town 8001, South Africa

14 Aquatic Drive
Frenchs Forest, NSW 2086, Australia

218 Lake Road
Northcote, Auckland

10 9 8 7 6 5 4 3 2

ISBN 1 85974 196 7 hb
ISBN 1 84330 170 9 pb

Publishing Manager: Jo Hemmings
Editor: Ian Kearey
Designer: Alan Marshall
Cartography: William Smuts
Index: Janet Dudley

Reproduction by Pica Digital Pte Ltd, Singapore
Printed and bound in Singapore by Tien Wah
Press (Pte) Ltd

First published in 1999 by New Holland
Publishers (UK) Ltd

Illustrations appearing in the preliminary pages
and on the last page are as follows:

HALF TITLE: An 'angel' at the Easter festival,
San José church, Las Piñas, Metro Manila.
FRONTISPIECE: Sunset over Cadlao Island,
El Nido, Palawan.
TITLE PAGE: A horse-drawn *calesa* in Vigan.
PAGE 4: The food market in Iloilo.
PAGE 5: A jeepney in Subic Bay.
PAGE 6: White Beach, Boracay.
PAGE 7: Dancers at the January Ati-Atihan
festival, Kalibo.
PAGE 176: Masskara festival masks, Bacolod.

ACKNOWLEDGEMENTS

The author/photographer and publishers would
particularly like to express their gratitude to the
following for their generous and valuable assis-
tance during the preparation of this book:

Eduardo Jarque Jr. and Madonna L. Noche,
Philippines Department of Tourism, London
Philippine Department of Tourism, the
Philippines: Legazpi, Davao, Tacloban and
Bacolod offices

Philippine Visitors and Convention
Corporation • Sorsogon Provincial Tourism
Promotion Council • Albay Provincial Tourism
Promotion and Development Office •
Shangri-La Hotels & Resorts in association
with Traders Hotel, Manila; Makati Shangri-La
Hotel, Manila; EDSA Plaza Shangri-La Hotel,
Manila and Shangri-La's Mactan Island
Resort, Cebu • Bacolod Convention Plaza
Hotel, Bacolod • Alona Tropical Resort, Alona
Beach, Bohol • Ten Knots Development
Corporation – Lagen Island Resort, El Nido,
Palawan • The Manila Hotel, Manila •
Grand Boulevard Hotel • Sea Breeze Lodge,
Coron, Palawan • Whitetip Divers, Manila •
La Laguna Beach Club & Dive Center, Puerto
Galera, Mindoro • Savedra Dive Center,
Moalboal, Cebu • Calypso Diving, Boracay •
Sea Dive Center, Coron, Palawan • Sea
Explorers, Dumaguete and Alona Beach
branches • Southern Cruise, Cebu •
Philippine Eagle Foundation Inc. • World
Wide Fund for Nature, the Philippines •
Department of Environment and Natural
Resources, Batanes Islands • Kitanglad
Integrated NGOs • The Natural History
Museum, University of the Philippines,
Los Banos • DDFE Resources

CONTENTS

Preface 7
Map of the Philippines 8

Profile of the Philippines 10

The Land 12 • The Wildlife 14 • The People 18
History 24 • Government 28 • Economy 29
Arts and Crafts 32 • Food and Drink 34 • The Regions 36

Journey through the Philippines 42

Around the Northern Islands 42
Coastal North Luzon

Through the Highland Mountains 56
The North Luzon Interior

The Heart of the Nation 68
Manila, South Luzon and Mindoro

The Land of Festivals 92
The Western Visayas

Gateway to the South 114
The Eastern Visayas

The Islands of the South 134
Mindanao and the Sulu Archipelago

An Unspoilt Outpost 156
Palawan

Index 174
Photographic Acknowledgements 176

PREFACE

For over a thousand years, the tropical archipelago of the Philippines – strategically placed between the South China Sea and the Pacific Ocean – has attracted traders, explorers, foreign powers and travellers from all over the world. Today, as an independent nation, we welcome thousands of visitors every year and share with them our country's diverse treasures: rugged mountains and lush green forests, idyllic palm-fringed beaches and colourful coral reefs, a unique cultural heritage, and the warmth of our people and their love of festivals and celebrations.

To travel through the Philippines is to experience both diversity and contrast at almost every turn. The remote island of Palawan, with its rich fauna and flora, is a world away from downtown Manila's modern streetlife bustle, while a jeepney trip to the magnificent, ancient rice terraces of Banaue provides a vastly different viewpoint to the leisurely lifestyle of Boracay, a beach thought by many to be the world's most beautiful. Our people, too, reflect diversity: over a hundred different cultural groups, many of whom still live according to the traditions of their forebears, combine in a blend of Eastern, Western and indigenous cultures to make up the population.

To capture on the printed page this vivid variety is no easy task. But just as the Philippines welcomes visitors to see for themselves all that the country has to offer, so readers of *This is the Philippines* will, through superb photographs and illuminating text, discover the wealth of riches that makes the Philippines so unique.

GCaraneta

Gemma Cruz-Araneta
Secretary of Tourism

THE PHILIPPINES

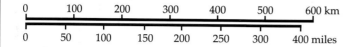

```
0        100      200      300      400      500    600 km
|---------|--------|--------|--------|--------|--------|

0     50    100    150    200    250    300    400 miles
|------|------|------|------|------|------|------|
```

```
Metres  0    200   500   1000  2000  3000

Feet    0    656   1640  3281  6562  9843
```
Height above sea level

JOURNEY THROUGH THE PHILIPPINES

The areas covered by the chapters
in **Journey through the Philippines**
are ordered according to the
following sequence.

1 Around the Northern Islands
Coastal North Luzon   **Pages 42-55**

2 Through the Highland Mountains
The North Luzon Interior   **Pages 56-67**

3 The Heart of the Nation
Manila, South Luzon and Mindoro   **Pages 68-91**

4 The Land of Festivals
The Western Visayas   **Pages 92-113**

5 Gateway to the South
The Eastern Visayas   **Pages 114-133**

6 The Islands of the South
Mindanao and the Sulu Archipelago   **Pages 134-155**

7 An Unspoilt Outpost
Palawan   **Pages 156-173**

N

MALAYSI

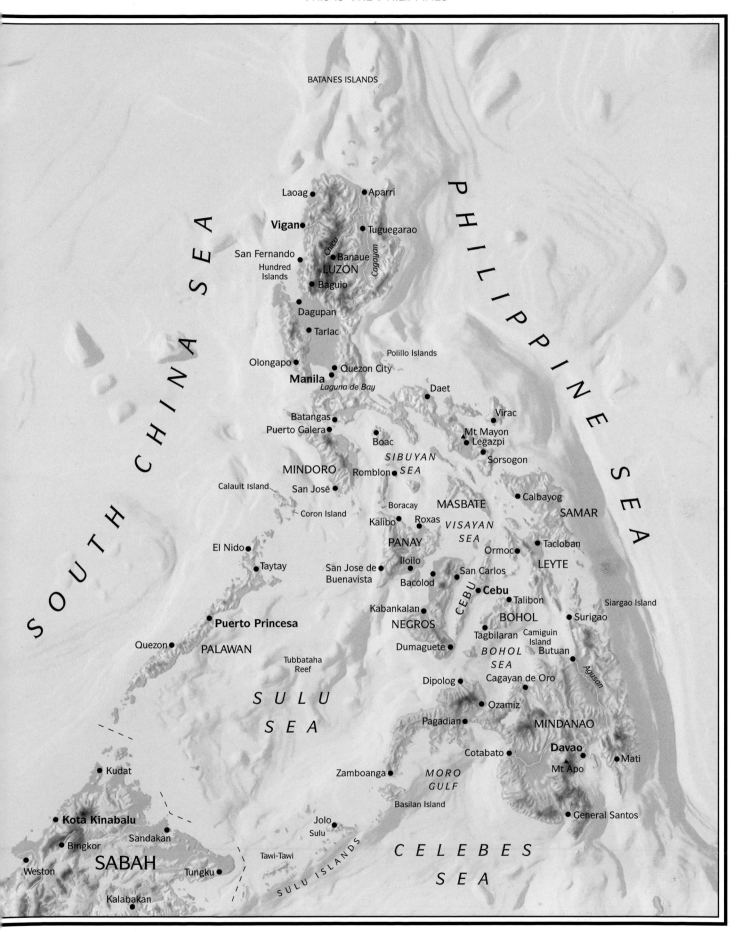

BATANES ISLANDS

SOUTH CHINA SEA

PHILIPPINE SEA

Laoag • • Aparri

Vigan • • Tuguegarao

San Fernando • *Chico* • Banaue • Tuguegarao

Hundred Islands LUZON *Cagayan*

• Baguio

Dagupan •

• Tarlac

Olongapo • Polillo Islands

• Quezon City

Manila • • Daet

Laguna de Bay

Batangas • Virac

Puerto Galera • Mt Mayon ▲

Boac • Legazpi

SIBUYAN SEA Sorsogon •

MINDORO Romblon •

Calauit Island San José • • Calbayog

Boracay • MASBATE SAMAR

Coron Island Kalibo • Roxas •

VISAYAN SEA

El Nido • PANAY Ormoc • • Tacloban

Taytay • Iloilo • LEYTE

San Jose de Buenavista • San Carlos •

Bacolod • **Cebu**

CEBU • Talibon Siargao Island

Kabankalan • BOHOL • Surigao

Puerto Princesa NEGROS Tagbilaran • Camiguin Island

Quezon • Dumaguete • *BOHOL SEA* Butuan •

PALAWAN Dipolog • Cagayan de Oro • *Agusan*

Tubbataha Reef Ozamiz •

SULU SEA Pagadian • MINDANAO

Cotabato • **Davao**

• Kudat Zamboanga • *MORO GULF* Mt Apo ▲ • Mati

Basilan Island

Kota Kinabalu Jolo • • General Santos

• Bingkor Sulu •

Sandakan • *CELEBES SEA*

Weston • SABAH Tawi-Tawi •

Tungku • *SULU ISLANDS*

Kalabakan •

PROFILE OF THE PHILIPPINES

With a skyline of smouldering volcanoes rising above lush tropical forests and a coastline of dazzling white beaches guarded by beautiful coral reefs, it is easy to understand why the Philippines is regarded as one of the world's most exotic countries, one shrouded in a little mystery by its rather isolated position on the eastern edge of Asia. An island nation, the country consists of a sprawling tropical archipelago, bordered by the Pacific Ocean to the east and the South China Sea to the west. It is claimed to consist of 7107 islands, though most of these are too tiny to be inhabited or even have an official name, and it is the ten largest islands that make up the overwhelming majority of the land area. These are host to an extraordinary range of landscapes: mountains and volcanoes, jungles and rainforests, plains and highlands, rivers and lakes, and in particular, some of the world's most beautiful beaches. Here the visitor can sail, surf and explore coral reefs, or soak up the sun while watching the fisher people bring in the day's catch in characteristic outrigger boats.

The Filipino people who live in these islands are closely related to the Malays of Indonesia and Malaysia, though their considerable diversity has given rise to a large number of ethnic groups. This diversity is reflected in the range of dialects spoken, as well as varying customs, that together have generated a rich cultural tapestry. This is further enhanced by overlays from several other cultures, principally Chinese, Spanish and American, the result in the first case of steady immigration over the past thousand years, and in the last two of 400 years of colonial rule. Perhaps the biggest single impact of Western occupation was the conversion of the Philippines into what to this day is Asia's only principally Christian country, something that, not surprisingly, has had a profound influence on the country's way of life. Nevertheless, since independence the Philippines has begun to assert its own unique identity. Today it is a country that combines stunning beauty with a charismatic blend of Malay and Western cultures, and offers a fascinating and intriguing destination for the traveller.

THE LAND

Sitting at the edge of island South-east Asia and surrounded by deep seas, the Philippines is very much a product of the geological forces of plate tectonics. The main islands are literally the peaks of submarine mountains driven upwards by forces generated as the rather small Philippine and vastly larger Eurasian plates drive against one another. The result is a rugged mountainous landscape, punctuated by volcanoes in areas where the Earth's crust has been weakened. Deep sea channels run between many of the mountain chains, creating the mountainous island archipelago, most of whose islands have probably never been linked by land bridges.

About two-thirds of the country's 300,000 square kilometres (115,200 square miles) of land is made up by the two main islands, Luzon and Mindanao, which form the main land masses in the north and south respectively. The central region consists of a fragmented mass of islands collectively known as the Visayas, whose main islands are Cebu, Negros, Panay, Bohol, Samar, Leyte, Romblon and Masbate. Taken together, they have a land area of just over 61,000 square kilometres (23,424 square miles). To the west lies Palawan, a cluster of 1,700 islands whose mainland is a long narrow island about 400 kilometres (250 miles) long and in places barely 8 kilometres (5 miles) wide, that points south-west towards Borneo. Finally, Mindoro is another island grouping, consisting mainly of the single mountainous island of Mindoro but also with several outer islands, that lies in the underbelly of southern Luzon.

Luzon, Mindanao, the Visayas, Palawan and Mindoro thus form the five main island groupings of the Philippines. However, there are a couple of other more remote island clusters that constitute the most isolated parts of this country. The first of these are the Sulu Islands, a long chain that consists mostly of the Basilan, Jolo and Tawi-Tawi island groupings, stretching south-west from the western extremity of Mindanao almost the whole way to Borneo. The furthest settlements in the Tawi-Tawi group are closer to Malaysia and Indonesia than they are even to Mindanao, let alone the Philippine heartlands of Luzon.

The second remote island cluster is the Batanes Islands. A group of ten tiny islands lying between the northernmost tip of Luzon and Taiwan, this is a wild, storm-battered landscape, its cliffs and rocky shores quite unlike anything seen elsewhere in the Philippines.

Most of the country's main mountain ranges run approximately north-south, something that is most easily seen in the northern half of Luzon, where three ranges, the Sierra Madre, the Cordillera Central and the Zambales Mountains,

Volcanoes are an ever-present fact of life in the Philippines. Here Mount Mayon (2421 metres/7941 feet), the country's most active volcano, towers over the city of Legaspi.

PREVIOUS PAGES
Page 10: *Traditionally dressed Bagobo dancers performing folk dances in Manila.*
Page 11: *A festival food stall at Iloilo, Panay.*

extend across much of the land. The highest peaks of the mountain ranges are mostly volcanoes: the country's two highest, for example, are Mount Apo (2954 metres/9689 feet) and Mount Dulang-Dulang (2938 metres/9637 feet) in the Kitanglad range, both inactive volcanoes in Mindanao. However, Mount Pulag (2930 metres/9610 feet) in the Cordillera Central, the highest mountain on Luzon and the third highest in the country, is not a volcano but the result of more gradual geological uplifting.

The tectonic plates that created the Philippines are still pushing the islands upwards, ensuring that earthquakes and volcanic eruptions are not completely consigned to the past. This firmly establishes the Philippines as a member of the Pacific Ring of Fire, and is responsible for a large proportion of the many volcanoes that encircle the Pacific from South and North America, to the Kamchatka peninsula, Japan, into the Philippines and Indonesia.

The Philippine islands contain 22 active volcanoes, with over 200 classed as inactive. The Philippine Institute of Volcanology and Seismology does not divide inactive volcanoes into dormant and extinct due to the extreme difficulty they have in deciding when a volcano really has breathed its last. Just about any of the inactive volcanoes could spring to life without warning, as was amply demonstrated by the 1991 eruption of Mount Pinatubo, a volcano that had lain inactive for 450 years.

The country's most active volcano is Mount Mayon, situated in the far south of Luzon, close to the city of Legaspi. It is famous for its almost perfect conical shape, its slopes sweeping upwards in a dramatic arc from the coast to the small, permanently smoking crater at the very summit. It is known to have erupted at least 44 times, on occasions with destructive results. An eruption in 1814 saw the village of Cagsawa swallowed up by lava flows, and in the most recent eruption, in 1993, over

70 farmers were killed and numerous buildings destroyed.

Without doubt the country's most infamous volcano is Mount Pinatubo, situated in the Zambales Mountains just 90 kilometres (55 miles) north-west of the capital, Manila. Inactive for 450 years, it exploded in June 1991 in one of the 20th century's biggest eruptions, sending ash and rock 30,000 metres (100,000 feet) into the air and turning day into night as far away as Manila. As the eruption subsided a typhoon swept through, causing massive avalanches that swept away entire villages and towns. Hundreds of people were killed, and hundreds of thousands were made homeless.

Because of the mountainous terrain, rivers in the Philippines are mostly short and swift. The longest, the Cagayan in northern Luzon, and the Agusan and Rio Grande de Mindanao in Mindanao, all flow through lowland areas originally created by the deposition of sediments over coral shelves. Both Mindanao rivers flow through vast marshes that remain vital wildlife refuges. Many of the coastal plains were also created by such sedimentation, which, in combination with the generally mountainous terrain, has created a highly indented coastline with many natural harbours; Manila Bay is perhaps the best known example of these.

While the main islands have been created by immense, sometimes violent geological forces, the small islands and islets have come about through a much gentler process: the growth of coral reefs. Reefs that were formed during geological periods when sea levels were higher than today, or which have been driven above sea level by tectonic forces, are today's coral atolls and islands. They are typically a dry landscape of brittle, heavily pitted and weirdly shaped limestone – the skeleton of old coral – which over the aeons has been worn down around the shore to produce stunning white beaches. On the oldest and largest of these islands enough soil has built up to allow quite extensive forest growth or cultivation, but on those islands with little soil, the vegetation is often sparse and highly specialized. The waters around such islands are usually very clear and are the sites of today's

Limestone islands formed over thousands of years from coral reefs can be found around many parts of the Philippine coasts; these are part of the Hundred Islands in Lingayen Gulf.

coral reefs. This is the basis for the Philippines' magnificent beaches, and it is no coincidence that the best occur on the smaller islands. It is here that desert islands are a reality – over 4000 of them are only known by local names – ringed by pristine beaches and crowded only with coconut palms.

CLIMATE

Lying at latitudes between 5° and 21° North, the Philippines has a tropical climate that is controlled by the north-east and south-west monsoons, the latter blowing from June to November, and the former throughout the rest of the year. The south-west monsoon, blowing from the Indian Ocean, brings warm but very wet weather to much of the country. The north-east monsoon, on the other hand, because it originates over the north Asian land mass, is rather drier and cooler. However, as it passes over the Western Pacific it does pick up some moisture, thus bringing rain to those areas most exposed to it, principally the east coasts.

The country is divided into five climatic zones, based on the annual periods of wet and dry weather, something largely determined by relative exposure to each of the monsoons, especially in the northern part

of the country. Thus, those areas exposed only to the south-west monsoon, such as the western half of Luzon, Mindoro and Palawan, have a dry period from December to May and heavy rain from June to November. Areas that are exposed mainly to the north-east monsoon, such as the Pacific coast, receive heavy rain from November to January, but also are subject to some rain during the south-west monsoon.

The regions that are exposed to, or sheltered from, both monsoons generally have rain distributed fairly evenly through the year, though clearly much more intensely in the case of the former. The only period when reasonably dry weather can be assured over most of the country is April–May, but these are in turn also the hottest months.

During the south-west monsoon typhoons sweep across the northern half of the country, travelling from the Pacific towards China or Vietnam. There are usually about 20 each year, bringing winds of over 150 km/hr (90 miles/hr) that batter the sparsely populated east coast, and cause extensive flooding in Manila. However, they rarely affect the southern part of the country, from a point just north of Cebu southwards.

13

Most of the Philippines' most spectacular beaches, such as Diniwid Beach on Boracay, are on the smaller offshore islands, and were created from the erosion of coral reefs.

Temperatures in the lowlands rarely drop below 26°C (79°F) even at night, and during the daytime they are almost always over 30°C (86°F). During May temperatures are often as high as 38°C (100°F). In the mountains, however, the temperatures rapidly drop; at about 1500 metres (4900 feet), for example, daytime temperatures are roughly equivalent to summer temperatures in many temperate regions. In the highest parts of the mountains, daytime temperatures may be comfortable, but the nights can be very cold, at about 4–8°C (39–46°F), and this can be accentuated by the damp atmosphere and high rainfall. On many of the small islands, despite quite high daytime temperatures, the nights can be pleasantly cool due to sea breezes.

THE WILDLIFE

The prolonged isolation of the Philippines, with no land bridges connecting it to the main Asian land masses in recent geological times, has meant that much of the country's wildlife has evolved quite separately from that in other parts of Southeast Asia, producing many unique forms. It has been estimated that over half of all species of Philippine fauna and flora are endemic, or unique, to the country. Two-thirds of the 180 species of mammal are unique, with a similar proportion for both amphibians and reptiles as well as plants. Among the 556 species of bird, 43 per cent live nowhere else. Because of these factors, the Philippines is recognized as one of the world's most important biodiversity hotspots.

TERRESTRIAL WILDLIFE

Until this century the Philippines was almost completely covered with tropical rainforest, and so much of its terrestrial wildlife is adapted for this habitat. One of its most well known endemic forest species is the Philippine Eagle, the world's second largest eagle, after the Harpy Eagle of South America. Despite the loss of its forest habitat, it continues to survive in remote areas of Mindanao and northeast Luzon.

Other species closely associated with the Philippine forests include the Philippine Tarsier, a tiny monkey-like animal, similar to the tarsier of Borneo, that lives in Mindanao and Bohol, and the Tamaraw, a species of wild buffalo that lives only on Mindoro. Most of the country's mammals are either rodents or bats, the latter including both the world's largest and smallest species. The largest bats, all fruit bats, include the endemic Philippine White-winged and Golden-crowned Flying Foxes, as well as a number of species that are spread across Southeast Asia. These bats, which generally have a wingspan of 1–2 metres (3–6 feet), are wholly vegetarian, feeding off forest and orchard fruits during the night. In the daytime they roost in high trees, usually forming colonies of up to several thousand animals. One of the most widespread mammals is the Long-Tailed Macaque, one of the few mammals that is common here and across South-east Asia.

Among the reptiles, monitor lizards are common, and two species of crocodile are present, mainly in marshes and mangroves: the Saltwater Crocodile, which is spread across much of tropical Asia, and the Freshwater or Philippine Crocodile, which is unique to the country.

In addition to the Philippine Eagle there is a great wealth of spectacular forest birds, including a number of parrots, such as the Blue-naped Parrot, and the Philippine Cockatoo. Flowerpeckers, woodpeckers, kingfishers and pigeons are all quite common, usually as several species, and many of them are very colourful. The Red Jungle Fowl, the ancestor of the domestic chicken, is also commonly encountered – or at least heard – in the forests.

Due to the deep water channels that separate many of the islands, species differences exist from one island grouping to the next. For example, there are at least four species of wild pig in the Philippines, each occupying a different part of the country. It is a similar story for deer, with the Philippine Spotted Deer restricted to just a few Visayan islands, and the Calamian Deer living only in the Calamian islands of northern Palawan. Even with birds these island differences apply: the bleeding-heart pigeons (so named for the splash of red on their breasts), for example, are divided into several species on different islands. Similarly, Philippine hornbills exist as distinct species

The Philippines' fauna and flora are as varied as they are unusual. Most animals have adapted to life in the forests, from the huge Philippine Eagle (above, near right) *to the tiny Philippine Tarsier* (below right). *The Bearcat, or Binturong* (below centre), *lives in the forests of Palawan and is found across much of South-east Asia. The tiny Olive-Breasted Sunbird* (below left) *can often be seen in gardens, feeding on the nectar of flowering shrubs and trees. Although orchids are found throughout the forests, their best displays are usually in private gardens* (above, far right), *as they are the main decoration around many homes.*

restricted to specific islands, such as the Sulu Hornbill, Palawan Hornbill and Visayan Wrinkled Hornbill.

The one part of the Philippines that has not been completely isolated is Palawan, which probably had a land bridge to Borneo at some point in the past. As a result, Palawan has a fauna and flora quite similar to that of Borneo, with numerous plants, mammals and birds found here and in other parts of South-east Asia, but which are completely absent from the main body of the Philippines. Examples include the Greater Mouse Deer, the Binturong (or Bearcat), the Asian Short-clawed Otter, the Pangolin and the Hill Myna. Nevertheless, there are a number of species that are restricted to Palawan, including the Palawan Hornbill and the Palawan Peacock Pheasant.

The Philippines sits astride one of the world's major biogeographic divisions, the Wallace Line, named after the 19th-century naturalist who discovered it. This line cuts through the Sulu Sea, which lies between Palawan and the rest of the Philippines. The areas to the west, including Palawan, have a mainly Asiatic flora and fauna, whereas to the east is a transitional zone called Wallacea, in which, as one moves eastwards, Australian species become increasingly abundant. With the exception of Palawan, the Philippines lies within Wallacea.

MARINE WILDLIFE
With over 1.6 million square kilometres (614,400 square miles) of sea, five times the land area, the Philippines has a rich diversity of marine life. The shores in many sheltered areas, such as bays and river estuaries, are covered with mangroves, specialized salt water-tolerant forests that harbour the young fry of a

The Philippines has one of the world's most spectacular submarine environments. Fish of all shapes, sizes and colours inhabit the reefs, including these Eye-patch Butterflyfish (top left). *In their undersea environment, beautiful gorgonian sea fans* (above right), *can often grow to a width of over two metres (six feet). On reefs adjacent to deep waters, especially in areas that are close to the open sea, several species of shark, including this Whitetip Reef Shark* (left), *are frequently encountered.*

great range of marine organisms, and so act as nurseries for a large proportion of the sea's life. Coral reefs perform a similar role along more exposed shores, and are themselves a massive living community. Philippine waters are said to contain about 34,000 square kilometres (13,000 square miles) of coral reefs, made up of 450 species of coral, a greater variety than is found almost anywhere else in the world. Moreover, a healthy reef will be adorned not just with a wide variety of corals, but also with sponges, anemones, tube worms, nudibranchs, sea cucumbers and starfish, in addition to huge numbers of reef fish, all of which depend on the reef for their shelter and food.

The fish found in these waters are enormously diverse and almost invariably colourful, from such delicate animals as the yellow and black butterflyfish or Moorish Idols, to the iridescent Blue or Green Wrasses. Equally eye-catching are the triggerfish, sweetlips (named for their pouting lips) and the triangular batfish. Reefs that lie close to deep water will also host shoals of barracuda, jack and tuna fish. Sharks, too, are quite common here, especially the Whitetip or Blacktip Reef varieties. The Philippine waters are also home to six species of marine turtle, including the Green, Olive Ridley and Hawksbill Turtles.

Whale Sharks, the world's largest fish, can be found in some areas. What is thought to be the world's largest concentration of Whale Sharks was recently discovered off the little town of Donsol, in southern Luzon. Here, about 50 sharks seem to spend most of their time along just a short stretch of coast, congregating here due to the high concentration of food. Despite their great size – they can grow up to 15 metres (50 feet) in length – Whale Sharks are plankton feeders and are therefore quite harmless to mammals or other sea-dwellers.

Over 20 species of whales and dolphins have been identified in Philippine waters, ranging from Sperm and Humpback Whales to Risso's and Spinner Dolphins. While these can in theory be seen just about anywhere around the Philippines, there are known concentrations in the waters off the south-west coast of Bohol, and at the southern end of the Tanon Strait, a narrow but extremely deep stretch of water that separates Negros from Cebu. Another rare marine mammal that can sometimes be encountered is the Dugong, which can be found in a very few areas around the coast of Palawan and southern Mindanao.

CONSERVATION

The Philippines developed one of the world's first protected areas systems, which was put in place during the early years of the 20th century by the American colonial administration. Unfortunately, this was not enough to protect the land from rapid deforestation and hunting, which between them have devastated large parts of the natural environment, bringing many species, including almost all those terrestrial animals described above, to the brink of extinction. Natural forest cover, which originally extended across more than 90 per cent of the country, has been greatly reduced, the result of commercial logging and slash-and-burn farming. Along the shores many mangrove areas have been cut down for firewood or to make way for fish and shrimp farms. At sea, over-fishing and the use of dynamite and cyanide have damaged corals, leaving only a minority of reefs unaffected.

Such environmental problems have an impact on both biodiversity and rural people. Deforested hillsides are not only prone to destructive landslides, but also rapidly lose their fertility with the eroding topsoil, which enters the rivers and kills the freshwater fish stock. Moreover, floods have become commonplace during the rainy season, and drought during the dry, resulting in a shortage of water. For the already struggling fishermen, a future on the land would offer few alternatives.

Since the late 1980s there has been a growing international effort to protect the remaining wild areas. Commercial logging has been banned, though it still continues on a small scale. Poverty and a rapidly

Conservation and the environment are becoming key issues in the Philippines. At Baclayon on Bohol Island, schoolchildren have been planting new mangrove trees across mud flats.

growing population ensure that slash-and-burn farming continues unabated and is now the main enemy of the forests. Many conservation groups are concentrating their efforts on helping the rural poor find ways to make a living that do not entail continually cutting down more forest. These include the cultivation and direct marketing of coffee and Manila hemp, permanent crops that can act as a valuable buffer between the human and natural environments.

With help from a number of international bodies and funding from the World Bank and the European Union, ten new priority protected areas (some of which were part of the old protected areas system), along with a range of secondary sites, have been set up in an effort to protect a sample of most of the Philippines' habitats. The whole of Palawan has been designated a protected area, within which specific national parks have been designated. In addition, many of the old pro-

tected areas that still contain valuable habitat are receiving a boost in the form of better financing and training for staff.

In the marine environment the long-standing bans on dynamite and cyanide fishing are now being enforced more effectively, though they remain a serious problem in some regions. Some of the major coral reefs have been designated national marine parks, and at the local level a large number of small marine sanctuaries have been established on healthier reefs to serve as seed banks to help re-establish healthy communities on nearby damaged reefs.

There are now many protected areas across the country; some of the most important of these, from the conservation viewpoint, are listed below:

Turtle Islands Wildlife Sanctuary, a group of very remote islands in the Sulu Sea, which are closer to Borneo than any of the Philippines' major islands. This priority protected area has been established due to its importance to nesting marine turtles, including the Green Turtle.

Mount Apo Natural Park is situated in southern Mindanao. This national park surrounds the country's highest peak, and at about 70,000 hectares (269 square miles) is one of the country's largest. Originally established in the 1930s, Mount Apo is also one of the new priority protected areas, for it is home not only to extensive forests but also to a wide range of animal species, including the Philippine Eagle. The climb to the summit is an increasingly popular challenge for hikers.

Agusan Marsh Wildlife Sanctuary, located in central Mindanao, is another of the priority protected areas, and is one of the country's largest remaining freshwater swamps. It is home to a unique kind of swamp forest, inhabited by a diverse array of wildlife, including the endangered Philippine Crocodile and Purple Heron.

Tubbataha Reef National Marine Park, a vast reef system isolated in the Sulu Sea, has one of the most spectacular undersea environments in the country. With a huge array of life that ranges from the tiniest reef fish to sharks, turtles and manta rays, this reef is thought to supply the bulk of the fish fry that supports virtually the entire Palawan fishing industry. For divers, this is one of the Philippines' best dive sites.

Olango Island, which is situated just east of Cebu, is a vast expanse of mud flats and mangroves that is the winter home to tens of thousands of migratory birds. The mangroves and scrubby woodlands that surround the marsh harbour a number of Philippine endemic species, so altogether this is a great place for birdwatchers to visit.

Sibuyan Island, a remote island in the northern part of the Visayas, has one of the country's largest remaining tracts of forest, which has survived due largely to the island's isolation.

Apo Reef Marine Wildlife Sanctuary, a large reef complex off the west coast of Mindoro, is a priority protected area that not only has a spectacular underwater world, but is also an important breeding ground for turtles on its islets.

Subic-Bataan Natural Park, which lies north-west of Manila, and part of which was protected in a US naval base until 1992, is one of the few remaining areas of lowland tropical rainforest left on Luzon, and for this reason is one of the new priority protected areas. The section of forest within the old naval base also represents some of the most accessible forest in the whole of the Philippines, being divided up by well laid and metalled roads. Wildlife here is quite approachable, making it easy to find macaques and a huge colony of fruit bats. Birdlife is prolific and quite readily seen.

Mount Pulag Natural Park protects the upper slopes of Luzon's highest mountain. Although serious incursions from surrounding farms have devastated most of its lower pine forests, the park still encloses an extensive mossy forest and a summit grassland rich in dwarf bamboo. The summit trail is a great climb for hikers.

Northern Sierra Madre Natural Park, also known as the Palanan Wilderness, is a priority protected area that lies in a remote region on Luzon's north-eastern Pacific coast, home to one of the country's last truly extensive tracts of rainforest. It also harbours the only Philippine Eagles known to live on Luzon.

The remote and isolated Tubbataha and Apo Reefs are good areas for viewing the Green Turtle, one of the six species of marine turtles which inhabit Philippine waters.

THE PEOPLE

The Filipinos of today are a rich blend of East and West. Essentially Malay people, they also have strong Chinese, Spanish and American influences in their make-up, a result of the many migrations and invasions that have washed over the country down the years.

The great majority of people are descended from Austronesians who migrated, probably from southern China or Taiwan, about 5000 years ago, and who were forebears not only of the Filipino people, but also the Malays of Indonesia and Malaysia, as well as the inhabitants of much of the Pacific. The Malays and Filipinos are thus believed to be derived from a common ancestor, which has given them similar physical characteristics and temperament. In some parts of the Philippines this similarity has been further increased by more recent immigrations of Malays from Borneo, Sumatra and Java, most of which occurred between the 11th and 16th centuries.

A pervasive Chinese influence has come about, mostly in the larger cities, as a result of repeated waves of immigration over the past thousand years by traders and refugees. Coming mainly from China's southern coastal provinces, they have contributed not only some physical characteristics but also food, a few aspects of language and names.

Today, while many people descended from the earlier migrants may be recognizable as Chinese only by their surname, descendants of 19th-century migrants and those who arrived after the communist takeover of China in 1949 still form a clearly defined group that maintains both its language and religion.

Centuries of colonial rule, mostly under the Spanish, but for 50 years under the United States, have also left an indelible mark. Spanish names abound, both in places and people, even though very few Filipinos today speak any Spanish. A few words and expressions have also entered the vernacular. Almost certainly the greatest Spanish influence has been to make the country Asia's only predominantly Christian one, with Roman Catholicism practised by over 80 per cent of people.

The Filipino people have diverse origins, from the Negritos (top left), *possibly the country's original inhabitants, to the Chinese (*top right). *The majority of the population consists of lowland Filipinos of* *Visayan or central Luzon origin* (bottom, left and right). *There is also a wide range of cultural minorities, including an extensive Malay Moslem influence, including the Yakan* (bottom, centre).

In their turn, the American colonialists introduced Protestantism, now followed by about 9 per cent of the population. They also developed within the country, especially the urban section of society, a love of the Western, especially American, lifestyle and a yearning for the 'American Dream'. This influence persists today in a general emulation of American styles, the huge numbers of American fast-food chains that line the streets and a high emigration to the USA; the last of these has resulted in close business and family ties between the two countries.

Undoubtedly one of the biggest American influences – and the most obvious to any visitor to the Philippines – is the widespread use of English, which persists as one of the country's three dominant languages. The importance of English is considered further below.

At the time of writing, the population stands at an estimated 72.6 million, a number that is growing at a staggering 2.3 per cent per year, one of the highest growth rates in the world. About two-thirds of these people live in the countryside, making a living from either the land or the sea. Of the 33 million urban dwellers, about a third live in the capital, Manila, which is by far the largest city in the country.

The rapidly growing population is a result of the strength of Catholicism, with its opposition to birth control, combined with a genuine love of children and a need among the poor to produce children as an insurance against their own destitution in old age. This has made it hard to implement a credible population programme. At the same time, it is creating serious problems, especially among the rural poor. Unequal distribution of land and lack of land tenure, combined with a declining productivity in both the land and sea, as well as fewer 'virgin' areas left to be opened up, have made it increasingly difficult for rural people to support their ever-

The Manobo live mainly in eastern Mindanao, including the waters of the Agusan Marsh Wildlife Sanctuary.

larger families. This has resulted in migration to the cities, especially Manila, leading to overcrowding and slum conditions for many.

At the other end of the social scale stand the elite families, mostly descen-

dants of those Spanish that held land during the colonial era, of Filipinos who played prominent roles in international trade and the plantation economies that developed during the 19th century, or of successful Chinese merchants and industrialists. This group consists of a relatively small number of people, but they have traditionally held the reins of power, and their control of the country's economy and government continues.

Between the two extremes stand the middle classes, mostly urbanized professional people, whose lives are not at all dissimilar from those of their counterparts in many other countries. One striking feature of Philippine society is the prominence of women. Although for the great majority having a family is a major goal, this does not prevent many women from obtaining senior and prominent positions in business and government. For the well-off, this is possible partly due to the widespread availability of domestic staff, employable at extremely low wages. For many, however, a major factor is the strength of the extended family, mothers being freed to work by the presence of grandparents, who are able to look after children during the daytime.

The strength of the family is one facet of society of which Filipinos are justifiably

The Ivatan inhabit the Batanes Islands, the northernmost outpost of the country, closer to Taiwan than the Philippine mainland.

proud. It is not simply a case of three generations living under the same roof, though that is part of it, but something encompassing strong ties of loyalty to a wider body of people, including aunts, uncles, cousins and even less closely related people. The result is a network of people able to help each other in times of need. In fact, more successful members of a family are duty-bound to help less well-off relatives if they ask. On occasion, strong family loyalties have led to accusations of corruption, with individuals abusing their positions of influence in order to improve the lot of their relatives.

CULTURAL MINORITIES

An estimated 10 per cent of the population belongs to one of the many cultural minorities. Depending on how one assesses cultural minorities, there are about 30 groups scattered around the country, mostly either in the mountainous areas of the north or in Mindanao and the Sulu Islands of the far south. Over the past 30 years many of the groups, especially those in Mindanao and Palawan, have had their traditional lifestyles greatly affected by an influx into their formerly sparsely

The Tagbanua, who live mainly in the Calamian Islands of northern Palawan, have traditionally been one of the shyest of the Philippines' cultural minorities.

populated territories of lowland Filipino settlers, an inevitable result of the growing population and declining resources in other areas.

Ethnologically speaking, one of the most important groups is the Negrito. Generally considered the original inhabitants of the Philippines, they are believed to be related to the Aborigines of Australia and to have migrated to this region as much as 60,000 years ago. Today, they continue to inhabit remote mountain regions of Negros, Panay and Luzon, often continuing their long-held forest hunter-gatherer existence, although they also farm in some areas. The Negrito go by a variety of names in different parts of the country, such as Ita, Ayta, Agta or Dumagat in Luzon, and Ati or Ata in Panay and Negros. The most accessible Negritos are probably those living in the forest within the old US naval base at Subic Bay. This is now open to visitors, and the inhabitants make a living by giving instruction in jungle survival skills and demonstrations of their lifestyle. Easily distinguished from other Filipinos by having extremely dark skin and tight curly hair, the Negrito population is believed to be slowly declining, their numbers now standing at about 15,000.

Similar in number are the Ivatans, who occupy the remote Batanes Islands that lie between the northernmost tip of Luzon and Taiwan. So cut-off are these people that there have been few strong outside influences since their ancestors, the Austronesians, landed here on their way south. To this day, they are believed to be pure Austronesian, speaking a language that is quite distinct from any heard elsewhere in the Philippines. The islands were not incorporated into the Spanish Philippines until late in the 18th century, and even then outside influence remained small, a state of affairs that continued under American rule. Many Ivatans continue with a traditional lifestyle, though with an increasing knowledge of the world around them some have opted to leave altogether, escaping the fierce storms that

Probably the best-known of the cultural minorities are the Ifugao, who live in northern Luzon's Cordillera Central.

sweep these islands much of the year in favour of the calmer climate of Mindanao.

The mountains of northern Luzon are occupied by a collection of cultural minorities, all people who have traditionally resisted outside control. These include the Apayao and Tingguian of Abra province, and the Ifugao, Kalinga, Bontoc, Ibaloi and Kalanguya, of Ifugao, Benguet and Mountain provinces. Some of these groups are especially well known for having been warlike headhunters in the past, and it has been reported that some of the remotest communities in parts of the Sierra Madre Mountains that border the Pacific coast still engage in ritual attacks on each other. There have even been rumours that, with a growing awareness of cultural identity, there has been a small-scale resumption of headhunting in one or two places. These people are not just traditionally warriors,

however, but also great agriculturalists; it was the Ifugao people who were responsible for constructing the astonishing rice terraces in and around Banaue about 2000 years ago, and today all these groups continue to farm the mountains as they have done for centuries.

Mindoro is known as the home of the Mangyan, a large group of about 30,000 people that is subdivided into nine subgroups, each speaking a different dialect. Believed to have migrated from Sumatra or Borneo 600–700 years ago, they still make up the bulk of Mindoro's rural population, practising slash-and-burn farming.

Quite an assortment of minorities live across Mindanao and the Sulu Islands, many of those in the western and far southern areas being Islamic. These Moslem groups include the Tausug (the main inhabitants of the Sulu Islands), Maguindanao, Maranao, Kolibugan, Yakan, Karaga, Sangil, Molbog, Jama Mapun and Samal.

A number of groups, however, retain traditional religious beliefs, especially those living in the eastern regions of Mindanao. These include the Manobo, Bagobo and Mandaya, while further west are the Subanon, Tasaday, Kulaman, Tagakaolo and T'boli. The last of these live around Lake Lanao, the country's second largest lake, and are well known for their colourful woven cloth.

The Badjao are a widely distributed group, living in the Sulu Islands, Palawan and Borneo. Often known as 'sea gypsies', these people live in boats or houses built on stilts over the sea. Their lives depend entirely on the sea, and they are master boatbuilders and seafarers. They are superstitious about the land, refusing to come ashore at night for fear of spirits.

In Palawan two of the main groups are the Pala'wan and Tagbanua. Many of the former continue to live traditional lives in the forests and hills of southern Palawan. The latter, numbering 8000–10000, live mainly in the Calamian Islands of the far north of Palawan. They are a rather shy and very peaceful group of farmers.

LANGUAGES AND DIALECTS

There are said to be about 80 dialects in the Philippines, though the vast majority of people speak one or more of the eight major tongues: Tagalog, Pangasinan, Pampangan, Ilocano, Bicol, Cebuano, Ilongo (also known as Hiligaynon) and Waray-Waray. The first four of these dialects are spoken mainly in Luzon, particularly the northern half, while Bicol is the dialect of southern Luzon. The other three are common in parts of the Visayas, Mindanao and Palawan.

Most dialects, including those of the cultural minorities, are derived from Austronesian, modified with varying degrees of influence from other languages such as Malay, southern Chinese dialects, ancient Indian tongues, Arabic and Spanish. The main Chinese dialects to be found are Fujianese and Cantonese, though the great majority of Filipino Chinese speakers are unable to read Chinese.

With such an array of languages and dialects, each associated with regional pride and loyalty, finding one that is universally understood and acceptable has in the past proved quite problematic. As a result, today there is just one national language, Pilipino, a consciously created tongue that is based on a standardized form of Tagalog. In actual fact, with 30 per cent of the population speaking Tagalog, including the residents of Manila, it is this language that has become the lingua franca in daily use, much to the dislike of the Cebuano and Hiligaynon speakers in the south.

The other Philippine lingua franca is English, a crucial relic of the American colonial era and one that reflects the pervasive influence of American culture, as mentioned above. Widely used in business and government, its use helps to placate opposition to the dominant role of Tagalog, providing a less politically charged alternative language.

English is a compulsory school subject, ensuring that it is spoken to at least a modest level even by the poorest fisherman. Many newspapers are published only in English, and most radio stations, even in the rural provinces, operate almost exclusively in this language, despite the fact that almost no one speaks it as their native tongue.

The central role of English ensures that anyone wishing to succeed in business or government must become quite fluent in the language. It is perfectly normal to hear educated Filipinos effortlessly, and perhaps a little confusingly, flip-flopping between English and Tagalog (or some other Philippine language), frequently mixing the two languages together in the same sentence.

Lighting candles at the Basilica Minore del Santo Niño in Cebu City. The majority of Filipinos are devout Catholics, and the churches are always occupied by people engaged in personal prayer.

RELIGIONS

As already mentioned, the most significant impact of foreign rule was the establishment of Christianity as the main religion. Today, an estimated 83 per cent of the population are Roman Catholics and 9 per cent are Protestants. Of the remaining 8 per cent, about half are Moslems and the remainder are a mixture of Buddhist or Taoist and animist.

The great majority of Filipinos are devout Catholics, with personal prayer and regular attendance at church mass of great importance. A large proportion of the churches in use date from the Spanish era, many of them solid, fortress-like structures built in a style known as 'Earthquake Baroque', constructed to withstand the twin depredations of earthquake and pirate attack. Many house historical and religious relics that go back to the earliest days of Spanish rule, and which are still shown great reverence. The oldest of these is the statue of the Santo Niño (infant Jesus), housed in Cebu's Basilica Minore del Santo Niño, which was given to the wife of local chief Humabon by Ferdinand Magellan in 1521. Another is the statue of the Black Nazarene, housed in Quiapo Church in northern Manila, a statue said to have been carved in Mexico and brought to the Philippines in the 17th century.

Protestantism mostly owes its origins in this country to the American colonial period, although much proselytizing by American groups continues today. In addition, there are two home-grown Christian groups, Iglesia ni Cristo and the Aglipayan or Philippine Independent Church. The former is a rather nationalistic Protestant group, established in 1914, whose churches are easily distinguished by their immensely modern and wholly uniform architecture, concrete structures with soaring spires and sweeping arches. The PIC is a Catholic group, established in 1888 as a protest against the domination of the church by Spanish priests, that to this day is independent from Rome.

Half of the country's non-Christians are Moslems, concentrated in the Sulu Islands and south-western Mindanao. Established in the region from the 13th century onwards, mainly as a result of trade with Moslem Chinese, Arabs and Islamized Malays from Borneo, these people have long resisted conquest and assimilation by the Christian majority. To this day, their culture remains quite distinct from that of the bulk of the Philippines.

The remaining 4 per cent of the population consists of a mixture of Buddhist or Taoist Chinese, while some of the cultural minorities are animists. Although some of the minorities have been Christianized, others have not. Examples of the latter include the Badjao, with their belief in land-based spirits, and the Manobo, for whom a supernatural world with a hierarchy of deities is linked to the human world by shamans. Other groups, even though supposedly Christianized, still maintain some aspects of their pre-Christian spirit beliefs, such as the carving of deity figurines to protect rice fields and homes against evil spirits. Even among the Catholic Filipinos, many aspects of folk religions survive, especially in a variety of superstitions and a belief in the power of talismans and shamans.

FESTIVALS

The Philippines could be called the land of festivals – there seems to be one happening somewhere every day. Every town and village has its annual fiesta, ostensibly to celebrate such events as the 'birthday' of their patron saint, the annual harvest of the main local agricultural crop, some historical or mythological event, or a combination of any of these. What is certain is that they represent the annual excuse for local people to forget all their daily troubles and really have a good time. Processions, church services, competitions, dancing and drinking are all essential parts of every festival, carried out with maximum gusto: Filipinos definitely know how to throw a good party!

One of the country's most spectacular festivals is Dinagyang, held each January in Iloilo. On the final day, teams put on dancing displays in a fierce competition to be acclaimed the best.

Originally encouraged by the Spanish to coincide with Christian holy days, the early festivals became vital tools in winning the people over to Christianity. Today, Christianity remains a major, if not the primary, force in most festivals. One of the most important is Cebu's Sinulog Festival, held in January, when the Santo Niño statue is paraded through the streets of Cebu City. Another is Manila's Festival of the Black Nazarene, also held in January, during which the Black Nazarene statue from Quiapo is carried through the streets. Rather more gruesome are the crucifixions that occur in several places on Good Friday, when a surprisingly large number of willing volunteers in search of penitence endure the pain of being scourged and nailed to a cross for up to several minutes. Probably the best-known of these bizarre crucifixions takes place near San Fernando in Pampanga province, north of Manila.

Events with a carnival atmosphere include the Ati-Atihan festivals of Panay, also held in January. Taking place in towns and villages all over the island, these festivals are said to celebrate a deal made between immigrating Malays (the ancestors of today's Panay people) and the local Negritos, which allowed the new arrivals to take control of large areas of land. The most famous of these festivals are Kalibo's Ati-Atihan and Iloilo's Dinagyang Festivals, huge events during which teams dressed in magnificent costumes dance through the streets. Kalibo's event is wild and chaotic, Iloilo's controlled and highly choreographed, but both are immense fun. Even these festivals incorporate a religious element, with statues of the Santo Niño paraded by some of the dance teams.

Other festivals, this time based on a local agricultural crop, include Camiguin Island's Lanzones Festival (held in October), to celebrate the harvest of the *lanzones* (lanson fruit), and Baguio's Flower Festival, held in February. At any time of year, a visitor travelling in rural areas for any length of time is certain to run into a local village fiesta. It is definitely worthwhile taking part in one of these events, as they are almost always friendly and enjoyable, and are definitely never to be forgotten.

HISTORY

The Philippines as an independent sovereign state is a very young country, the past 400 years of its history consisting almost entirely of its role as a colony of one of Europe's most powerful nations. What life was like here before the Spanish invasion has long been shrouded in mystery. Only in recent years has a picture started to emerge, of autonomous clusters

Near the North Luzon town of Banaue, the rice terraces, with their sophisticated irrigation systems, have been maintained for over 2000 years by the Ifugao people who built them.

of settlements and islands loosely linked into the great trading networks that existed in east Asia hundreds of years before the Europeans arrived on the scene.

THE BEGINNINGS
The earliest signs of human life go back 750,000 years to finds made in the Cagayan valley in the far north. It is likely, however that these were left by *Homo erectus*, the predecessor of modern humankind, *Homo sapiens*. The first signs of the latter date to 30,000–60,000 years ago, mainly from the Tabon Cave in Palawan. It is believed that these early people were related to today's Negritos, and it is on evidence such as this that the Negritos are generally accepted as being the Philippines' original inhabitants.

The Austronesians, the ancestors of the majority of today's Filipinos, arrived about 5000 years ago, in the early stages of their southward migration from Taiwan or southern China. They brought with them agricultural skills, in particular rice cultivation, which has formed the basis of Filipino life ever since. It is believed that the agricultural Austronesians and hunter-gatherer Negritos lived quite close to one another relatively peacefully, each benefitting from the other's skills. Inevitably, the settled agricultural lifestyle of the former led to their domination and continued expansion, further waves of migration leading to Austronesian settlement of all the islands of South-east Asia and many of those of the Pacific.

THE EARLY PHILIPPINES
No central power arose to make the Philippines a single country. Instead, the people lived in autonomous clusters of villages, or *barangay*, each with its own chieftain. In time, some places became important trading centres, often outposts of the Indianized empires of South-east Asia. These places became tied into the developing Asian maritime trade routes very early on. There is evidence, for example, of trade between the Philippines and Cham (in today's Vietnam) in 500BC.

Records for China's largest port, Quanzhou, situated on the coast of Fujian province, show that by the 10th century Filipino merchants were sailing regularly to China for business. Moreover, throughout China's Song and Yuan dynasties (960–1368) Chinese ships traded extensively with the Philippines, resulting in the establishment of permanent Chinese communities at a number of sites around the coast. Large finds of Chinese pottery and coins indicate that the main Philippine trading centres were at Butuan (on the north coast of Mindanao), Cebu (today the Philippines' second most important city), Tondo (a district in today's Manila) and the Sulu Islands.

Traders and immigrants also came from the south, mainly Borneo, but also Java and Sumatra. The most famous of the Malay immigrations is undoubtedly that of the Ten Datus (Malay chieftains), who are said to have fled with all their people from persecution in Borneo. They landed on Panay, where they were able to reach an agreement with the local Negritos to take over large parcels of land. The ten groups subsequently took over large areas of Panay and southern Luzon, becoming the ancestors of today's inhabitants of these regions. There were other Malay immigrations: the Mangyan people of Mindoro, for example, probably were derived from such an immigration 600–700 years ago.

From the 13th century onwards Arab missionaries began to arrive in the Sulu Islands aboard Chinese ships, starting the Islamization of the south-west. Sulu's first Islamic sultanate was established in 1450 under Sayyid Abu Bakr, a refugee prince from Sumatra. Islam then spread northwards into Mindanao, the sultanate of Maguindanao being established at the end of the 15th century.

At this time Tondo, sitting on the northern shore of the Pasig River, roughly in the area of today's Binondo district of Manila, came under the control of the Brunei empire. Many Malays and Chinese settled here, forming the nucleus of modern Manila's Chinatown. Brunei also established a settlement on the southern shore of the Pasig, right at the river's mouth, which was possibly called Maynilad, the predecessor of today's Manila. Both settlements, which became Islamized in the middle of the 16th century, were major trading centres, linking South-east Asia with China, and were thus of great importance to those who aimed to control international business.

THE ARRIVAL OF THE SPANISH

Ferdinand Magellan, a Portuguese working in the service of Spain, left Spain in 1519

The Magellan Cross stands in a pavilion in central Cebu City, on the spot where it is believed Ferdinand Magellan set up a cross when he arrived in Cebu in April 1521.

intent on finding a route to the Spice Islands, today's Moluccas in Indonesia. He set off with five ships, though he soon lost two, and sailed around Cape Horn, eventually reaching the Philippines. He and his men arrived off the coast of Samar on 16 March 1521. Their first landfall was on Homonhon, an island just south of Samar, and from here they sailed to Limasawa, and then to the trading port of Cebu, where they arrived on 7 April. The chief of Cebu, Rajah Humabon, was remarkably friendly, and within days Magellan had baptized him and many of his followers.

Magellan then made a fatal mistake. Lapu-Lapu, chief of Mactan Island, which lies next to Cebu, was in a dispute with his neighbour Humabon, something that Magellan decided to settle with a fight. With the Europeans heavily outnumbered,

their firearms proved insufficient to win the battle, and on 27 April Magellan was killed. Shortly afterwards many of his officers were massacred by Humabon's men, the survivors fleeing aboard their ships. Over a year later, 18 survivors out of the original 265 returned to Spain. Today, Lapu-Lapu is hailed as the first Filipino to repulse foreign aggression.

Between 1523 and 1546 Spain sent three more expeditions, and by the 1550s the islands had become known to the Spanish as Islas Filipinas, in honour of King Philip II of Spain. But it was not until 1565 and an expedition led by Miguel de Legaspi that Spain started to gain a hold on the Philippines. In that year Legaspi set up the first permanent Spanish settlement, in Cebu, though fears of an attack by the Portuguese soon led him to move to Panay.

In 1569 it was decided to attack Manila, a force from Panay arriving off the settlement in May 1570. After some initial friendly contact fighting started, as a result of which Manila was burned to ruins. Despite their victory the Spanish withdrew to Panay, only to return in May 1571, and this time the Malay leader, Rajah Soleiman, surrendered. The Spanish city of Manila was born, the new capital of what was to become Spanish-controlled Philippines, built on the ruins of the Malay settlement of Maynilad. From a simple wooden enclosure, attacks by the Chinese pirate Li Mahong and repeated fires led to its development as a highly fortified stone city, the Intramuros that can still be seen today. From this time until 1898 the Spanish were to rule the Philippines with only one interruption, a relatively brief occupation of Manila by British forces from 1762 to 1764.

SPANISH RULE

The Spanish extended their influence throughout lowland Luzon and the Visayas. Catholic priests were able to convert the Filipinos in their tens of thou-

Vigan is the best-preserved Spanish town in the Philippines. The entire district is lined with old Castilian houses, and horse-drawn carriages are the normal means of transport.

sands, greatly easing the spread of Spanish control. To govern the population, the many scattered settlements were compressed into towns and villages built around a church. The Spanish religious

Manila's Fort Santiago protected both the mouth of the Pasig River and Intramuros, capital of the Spanish Philippines.

authorities also took it upon themselves to destroy everything they could of the pre-Hispanic era. They did a very thorough job, wiping out records of life before their arrival and completely doing away with the native alphabet, a script known to be very similar to those of Java and Sumatra.

The *encomienda* system, first tried out in Spain's Central and South American colonies, was introduced. Parcels of land and all that stood on them – including the people – were awarded to men who had faithfully served the Spanish crown. The *encomiendero* was able to exact taxes and loyalty from the people on 'his' land, and was supposed to give protection in return. However, this was usually abused, leading to gross exploitation. It was the start of absentee landlordism, with the establishment of huge estates and the concentration of land, and hence power, into the hands of a few. To this day, such land-ownership patterns persist in many parts of the country, although government has pledged its support for land reform.

On the trade side, one of the most famous developments was the Manila Galleons, the annual sailing of a ship from Manila to Acapulco in Mexico, loaded up with trade goods and treasure. The annual event began early in the city's life and continued until 1815, but although the

trade made a few people immensely rich it was of no benefit to the country as a whole. Ironically, the success of this trade depended on the Chinese community, thanks to their vast web of connections right across South-east Asia, which could easily facilitate the flow of goods to and from Manila. The Chinese became an essential part of the economy, though they were mistrusted by the Spanish, who refused to allow them to enter Intramuros. Instead, they were forced to live on the banks of the Pasig River, within range of the walled city's guns.

REBELLION AND REVOLUTION

From the earliest days of Spain's occupation, rebellions against the rulers were common. The most famous of the early uprisings were those in the far north, led by husband and wife Diego and Gabriela Silang, though for a truly successful rebellion we need to look at Bohol. In 1744 Francisco Dagohoy succeeded in wresting independence for the island, which lasted until 1829, when the Spanish finally managed to re-invade.

During the 19th century European liberal ideas of democracy spread to the Philippines via Filipinos who had studied in Europe. These men campaigned for democracy at home, one of the foremost of whom was José Rizal (1861–96). His two novels, *Noli me Tangere* (Touch Me Not) and *El Filibusterismo* (Subversion) exposed the corruption of the Spanish Philippine government and predicted a revolution. His books were banned in the Philippines, and after returning home he was exiled to Mindanao.

While Rizal favoured peaceful change, others were for open rebellion. In 1892 Andres Bonifacio formed the Katipunan, an organization dedicated to the violent overthrow of the Spanish. Its membership grew by tens of thousands, and when the government discovered its secret network in 1896 Bonifacio launched the revolution. Rizal was accused of involvement, and after a show trial was executed on the edge of what is now Rizal Park, outside Intramuros, on 30 December 1896. The Revolution had its greatest martyr.

Fighting went on for several months, during which time an internal struggle broke out within the Katipunan, resulting in the execution of Bonifacio and the emergence of a new leader, Emilio Aguinaldo. Despite this, the Spanish were unable to put the revolution down, but neither could the Filipinos defeat the Spanish. At the end of 1897 a truce was agreed, with the leaders of the revolution going into exile in Hong Kong.

THE AMERICAN INVASION

Peace did not last long, however, at least in part due to the outbreak of the Spanish-American War, which resulted from a dispute over Cuba. The USA made plans to invade the Philippines and encouraged the exiles to return home. In May 1898 combined American and Filipino forces laid siege to Manila, and on 12 June the new Philippine government under Aguinaldo declared independence. Freedom was short-lived. The Spanish agreed to surrender, but only to the Americans and only with a face-saving mock battle that excluded the Filipino forces. In this way the Americans took Manila on 13 August, with Aguinaldo and his men frozen out.

Any doubts over the USA's intentions towards the country were dispelled by the Treaty of Paris, signed in December 1898, in which the USA bought the Philippines from Spain for US$20 million. The Filipinos were soon at war with their new masters, but it was a one-sided fight that ended in Aguinaldo's capture.

The early years of the USA's occupation were marked by the occasional brutal suppression of an uprising, but overall the government quickly became relatively benign. The elite of Philippine society were easily persuaded to cooperate, and by the 1910s a US-style congress was established; this was largely controlled by wealthy Filipinos, but its powers could be vetoed by the American governor.

The possibility of total independence was raised as early as 1916, but a change in US policy in the early 1920s led to an indefinite delay in steps down that road. However, by early 1933 it had been agreed that the Philippines would pass through a commonwealth phase, starting in 1935 and culminating in full independence on 4 July 1946. On 8 February 1935 the Commonwealth of the Philippines was inaugurated, with Manuel Quezon as President.

WORLD WAR II

Preparations for full independence were smashed in December 1941, when the Japanese bombed Pearl Harbor. Within hours American bases in the Philippines were bombed, and before the year's end, Manila. During December Japanese forces landed in several places in the Philippines, leading the outnumbered American forces, along with members of the Philippine government, to retreat to Corregidor Island and the Bataan peninsula in the mouth of Manila Bay. The Japanese entered Manila unopposed on 2 January 1942.

The besieged US-Filipino force held out for several months, though once Manuel Quezon and the US commander, Douglas MacArthur, had been ordered to leave and had escaped to Australia, resistance weakened. Bataan surrendered in April 1942, followed by Corregidor in May.

There followed three years of Japanese rule, which were characterized by continual guerrilla warfare against the occupiers. By 1944, however, the Americans were back, US forces under MacArthur landing on Red Beach on the east coast of Leyte on 20 October. Further landings on Mindoro in

The Rizal Monument in Manila was erected on the site where national hero José Rizal was executed in December 1896.

December, and then in the Lingayen Gulf north of Manila in January 1945 brought the US to within striking distance of the capital. After heavy fighting, Manila fell on 3 February 1945.

The Provincial Capitol building in Tacloban, Leyte, is decorated with a frieze depicting the landing of American forces at nearby Red Beach in October 1944, led by General Douglas MacArthur. The town celebrates the landing every October.

Independence Day is celebrated on 12 June, and as part of the national holiday, the Philippine army engages in a full-dress uniform march-past in Rizal Park, Manila.

INDEPENDENCE

Despite the devastation wrought by World War II, the country gained independence from the US on 4 July 1946. The first President of the new republic of the Philippines was Manuel Roxas.

Since then the Philippines has remained closely allied with the USA. The country became a major bastion in the West's fight against the spread of communism, numerous American bases being maintained across the country. The most important of these were the naval base at Subic Bay and the nearby Clark Air Force Base, both of which saw extensive service during the Vietnam War. The presence of the US military became a sovereignty issue, however, and when the 1991 eruption of Mount Pinatubo caused massive damage to Subic and Clark it became relatively simple for the Philippine Congress to ask the Americans to leave. The US finally pulled out in 1992.

For most of the postwar years the Philippines has remained democratic, with the exception of the Marcos period. Ferdinand Marcos was elected President in 1965 on a wave of optimism that he would provide a fairer distribution of the country's wealth. He was popular for the first few years, but when he declared martial law in 1972 it was done solely to maintain his grip on power. The next few years were marked by oppression, corruption and a massive siphoning-off of the country's wealth.

By the early 1980s the country was nearly bankrupt, and when Benigno Aquino, a popular opposition politician, was assassinated in 1983 as he was stepping off an airplane at Manila Airport upon return from exile, the end was near for Marcos. An election in February 1986 saw all the opposition parties back Aquino's widow, Corazon Aquino, in a joint move to push Marcos out. The vote clearly went in her favour, but Marcos claimed victory and held onto power anyway.

A military coup followed but failed, and as army units loyal to Marcos moved to attack the rebels the Archbishop of Manila, Cardinal Jaime Sin, called on the people of Manila to come to their protection. Hundreds of thousands of people turned out, blocking the path of the government forces and daring them to open fire on unarmed civilians. The US flew Marcos out to exile, and the People's Power Revolution had won. Corazon Aquino became the next president.

A new constitution was written, and the country was gradually put back on its feet. But Aquino was not a skilled leader. She failed to tackle many of the underlying causes of poverty and was unable to stimulate the economy. Discontent soared, leading to numerous insurrections and at least seven attempted military coups. By the late 1980s the communist New People's Army (NPA) controlled large parts of the countryside, especially on Mindanao, where the situation was compounded by Islamic separatists, mainly the Moro National Liberation Front (MNLF).

In 1992 an election gave the presidency to Fidel Ramos. He made peace deals with the NPA and MNLF, quickly moved to improve the atmosphere for foreign investment and set in motion a programme, called Philippines 2000, to industrialize the country and boost levels of education and training by the end of the century. By the late 1990s the economy was turning around, going from one of the worst in Asia to one of its most rapidly growing. Guerrilla activity is now a thing of the past for most of the country, with both town and countryside at peace. Problems remain, however, in western Mindanao and the Sulu Islands, where two Islamic separatist groups, Abu Sayyaf and the Moro Islamic Liberation Front (MILF), remain active. The Sulu Islands also suffer from occasional piracy.

Despite the massive improvements, poverty is still widespread and frustration at the slow pace of land reform is simmering. The NPA still exists, and could easily become a force to be reckoned with once again if conditions for the rural poor do not improve. It remains to be seen whether the President elected in May 1998, Joseph Estrada, will be able to deliver on his pledge to provide a better deal for the country's poor.

GOVERNMENT

The Philippines is a republic, which, with the well-publicized exception of the martial law years of the Marcos era (1972–86), has maintained a democratic system of government since independence. Apart from not being a federal country, the government system is modelled on that of the USA, with an elected president who holds the position of chief executive, and a bicameral Congress.

The latter consists of a Senate and House of Representatives, with 24 and 200 elected members respectively. The president is elected every six years, and in a bid to prevent a repeat of the Marcos era, is allowed to serve for only one term. Members of the Senate also sit for six years, though elections take place every three years, with half of the seats being voted on each time. Would-be senators stand for election at a national level, with no regional representation.

Regional representation occurs in the House of Representatives, the country being divided into constituencies, with the number of members elected from each constituency depending on its population. The entire House of Representatives is re-elected every three years, and each member is allowed to sit for three terms. Voting is by universal franchise.

There are a number of political parties, some of which are coalitions of smaller parties brought together to increase their power. The most important are Lakas-NUCD-UMDP-Nacionalista Party (usually known simply as Lakas), Laban Ng Makabayang Masang Pilipino (LAMMP) and the National People's Coalition (NPC). As of 1998, the current President, Joseph Estrada, is a member of LAMMP.

Politicians quite frequently switch from one party to another, and although professed party policies may differ quite markedly, in general the parties cannot be pigeon-holed as being, say, left-wing or right-wing. Furthermore, for the Philippine electorate the politicians' individual personalities and promises are often more important than what their parties stand for, and television and film celebrities who stand for election often have a good chance of winning.

Of particular importance to the outcome of elections are regional loyalties, a national politician almost certainly being able to count on the votes of the great bulk of people living in his or her home area. During presidential election campaigns, for example, a presidential candidate may choose their vice-presidential running mate not so much on any shared ideology or even personal compatibility but on their relative abilities to deliver bulk regional votes, such as the 'Visayan vote' or the 'northern Luzon vote'.

At an historical level, this regionalism can be seen in the reputations of the Marcos family. Though today they are reviled by the majority of Filipinos, in their home areas (Ilocos Norte in the north of Luzon for Ferdinand Marcos, and Leyte for his wife Imelda) they are still heroes who cannot be criticized.

Below the national level are three layers of local government, namely provincial, municipal and *barangay*, whose officials are all elected. Each is headed by a governor, mayor and *barangay* captain respectively, serving with their own elected assemblies, each in turn named the board, *sanguniang* and council. The *barangay* officials serve for five years, those at the municipal and provincial levels for three.

Though this is a highly democratic system, it is open to abuse at all levels. In the past, vote-buying by politicians has been quite common, as have such tricks as multiple voting by the same individual under different names, ballot box stuffing and intimidation of voters. Loyalty to, or even fear of, employers, major landlords (especially in agricultural areas) and traditionally powerful families has led voters to support the 'correct' candidate, especially at local government elections. Rumours of fraud and corruption abound, and occasionally politicians or their supporters have been arrested and charged. At national elections great efforts are going into minimizing such problems, and as the voting population slowly becomes more politically aware it is to be hoped that the electoral system will improve. In those few areas of the country still subject to guerrilla activity violence is not uncommon, although in most of the country today elections usually pass off peacefully.

ECONOMY

Since the mid-1990s the economy has been recovering rapidly from the devastation caused by the Marcos years. Annual growth in gross domestic product (GDP) has been at 5–6 per cent, and even with the Asian financial crisis which started in 1997, the economy has continued to grow, albeit at a much reduced rate,

In the bustling streets of Binondo, in northern Manila, the market stalls vie for attention with posters and placards of political candidates.

The mouth of the Agno River, near Lingayen in central Luzon, is a prime site for catching fish, and is usually crowded with rafts, each of which is fitted with a net that can be raised and lowered on a bamboo crane.

The mighty coconut palm is one of the kingpins of the rural economy, providing everything from timber to coconut oil.

despite a 40 per cent drop in the value of the country's currency, the peso.

Whilst moving towards industrialization, the country remains heavily dependent on the primary commodity products of fishing, agriculture and mining, areas where products are liable to suffer wide swings in value. About half of the country's population is still employed in fishing and agriculture, from small slash-and-burn plots on the upland forest margins to the vast sugar cane estates of Negros or the pineapple plantations of Mindanao. For these people wages are often extremely low, and this fact ensures a constant flow of migrants seeking opportunities in the big cities, where wages (and prices) are considerably higher.

AGRICULTURE

The principal agricultural crops are rice, corn (maize), sugar cane, pineapple, coconut and banana. The most important of these is rice, this one crop alone accounting for 20 per cent of all agricultural output, and taking up an estimated 3.2 million hectares (8 million acres) of land. As with most Asian countries, rice

forms the backbone of the diet, each Filipino eating an average of 100 kilograms (220 pounds) per year, contributing 35 per cent of calorie intake. To meet the needs of a rapidly growing population, the country is sometimes obliged to import rice from elsewhere. To avoid the major cost of this exercise, and to improve national food security, the International Rice Research Institute, based near Los Banos, is constantly working to find ways to boost rice yields.

Coconut is probably the country's main plantation crop, with a staggering 285 million palms spread across much of the country and occupying a similar land area to that of rice cultivation. It is difficult to think of a crop more versatile than the coconut: eating its flesh and drinking its milk are just the tip of the iceberg, for there is a whole host of products of immense use both in the local agricultural economy and the global industrial one. Not only is the timber of immense value, but also the nuts themselves have a range of uses that include the production of coconut oils, copra, coir (for mats and ropes), charcoal, activated carbon, vine-

gar, plant culture media, growth hormones (used in various food processing industries), laundry soap and detergents. In the case of coconut oil, for example, Filipino palms account for two-thirds of the world's entire production, 80 per cent of it exported to Europe and North America.

One of the major problems in the agricultural sector is the inequitable distribution of land, with vast areas in the hands of a few people – a leftover from the Spanish *encomienda* system – and large numbers of people with no secure land tenure anywhere.

Lack of access to the fertile lowlands, mostly already in the hands of large landowners, is one important factor forcing the growing population onto ever more marginal forest land, ensuring that they are never able to occupy a piece of productive land that they can call their own with any degree of certainty. Without land tenure and the documents to prove it, most of these people are unable to obtain the bank loans or credit that could help them escape the poverty trap. Successive governments have promised extensive land reform to help rectify this inequality, but progress in most parts of the country has been very slow. One encouraging development has been the growing success of a number of non-government organizations (NGOs) in setting up a variety of agricultural coops and micro-credit schemes among the rural poor.

MINING

The Philippines is rich in a variety of minerals, including copper, magnesium, manganese, zinc, iron ore, cobalt, gold and silver, and so it is not surprising that mining is one of the country's biggest export earners. The world's largest copper mine is on the west coast of Cebu, with other massive mines on the islands of Negros and Marinduque, and the Philippines is South-east Asia's largest producer of this metal. Significant amounts of gold and silver are also mined, the most productive areas being in the Cordillera Central mountains of northern Luzon, especially around Baguio, although there are also mines on Mindanao. The negative side-effect of so much mining is extensive pollution. Furthermore, the mining industry is a ready source of explosives and cyanide (the latter used in the extraction of gold), which frequently find their way into illegal and destructive fishing methods at sea.

INDUSTRY AND PHILIPPINES 2000

Industrial products include food processing, textiles and electrical and electronic goods. With the introduction of Philippines 2000, a programme to industrialize the country by the start of the Millennium, this is the fastest growing sector of the economy, though most industrializing areas are concentrated around Manila, Cebu and the two economic zones, at Subic Bay and Clark Field.

Another component of Philippines 2000 is a boost to the education system, since one of the country's major problems is the shortage of a highly skilled workforce. Thanks to an effective primary education system, the Philippines enjoys a high national literacy rate of about 95 per cent. Once education at higher levels has begun to catch up, the country can look forward to generating a competitive industrial economy capable of ending widespread poverty.

A new industrial zone at the old American Subic Bay naval base, now called Subic Bay Freeport. Although agriculture is still the biggest employer in the Philippines, industry is the fastest growing sector of the economy.

Due to the difficulty in finding adequate work at home, hundreds of thousands of Filipinos travel overseas every year, often leaving behind close relatives, even spouses and children, for years on end. Many find the pain of separation worthwhile, as even menial work overseas will generally ensure a wage vastly greater than any available in the Philippines.

Many thousands of women, from teenagers upwards, find work as domestic staff in homes across east Asia, particularly in Hong Kong, as well as in the USA and these days even Western Europe, while Filipino workers are common in the Middle East's oil industry and the world's merchant shipping.

The remittances that these people are able to send home make a significant contribution, not only to the country's foreign currency earnings but also to the ability of their families to survive. On their eventual return to the Philippines the *balikbayan*, as those returning from overseas work are called, hope to have saved up enough money to set themselves up in a reasonable business that will support themselves and their family for the rest of their lives.

Improvements in the Philippine economy in the early 1990s saw a property boom in Manila, leading to the construction of many new high-rise buildings.

Today's Philippine dance theatre is an eclectic mix of styles, embracing both ancient tribal dance rites, for instance depicting the relationship between a mother and daughter (left), and elegant dances of Spanish origin (below left), which were popularized in the Philippines during the 19th century. The accompanying musical instruments show the same influences, from the percussion orchestras typical of South-east Asia to the descendants of European stringed instruments (below right).

ARTS AND CRAFTS

The long colonial period to which the Philippines was subjected not surprisingly had a profound effect on the country's arts, all but smothering native styles and images and replacing them with Christianized European forms. Since the first half of this century, however, there has been a steady search for a national identity, from literature and the plastic arts, through music, to dance and drama, resulting in the emergence of a unique and exciting mix of modern and traditional, Western and Filipino.

Traditional Filipino dance styles are derived from pre-Hispanic practices and are based largely on the agricultural cycle. Many stylize rice planting or harvesting, fishing or hunting, for example, while oth-

ers enact scenes from epic stories or are based on traditional tribal rites and ceremonies. These were preserved during the colonial era largely by the tribal groups who resisted Spanish control, and were incorporated into dance performances following research begun in the 1930s by Francisca Reyes Aquino, a member of the University of the Philippines Folk Song and Dance Troupe. This has led to a massive revival of these tribal dance forms, with a number of dance groups that regularly perform them.

It is usual for these dances to be performed alongside others derived from the Spanish and American eras, as well as from the Islamic south. The first of these are European in both dress and style, having grown in popularity among the wealthy classes in the 19th century, while the

American dances have a distinctly vaudeville flavour to them. The Islamic dances, clearly Malay in character and with stunningly exotic costumes, generally enact scenes from Malay epic tales. A visit to a dance performance of the kind often staged in Manila's Intramuros or Rizal Park is to experience an eclectic mix of highly contrasting dance styles from East and West, all integrated into what is now thought of as Filipino style.

The musical instruments used at such a performance also reveal these extreme mixes, the switch from Malay or Filipino tribal to Spanish or American dance styles signalling the need for the accompanying group of musicians to change seamlessly from the classically South-east Asian gongs and bamboo instruments to the Spanish guitar and violin.

Folk art in the Philippines is used for decoration, social identity and propaganda. Close to the Rizal Monument in Manila's Rizal Park are a number of murals (right), *depicting the unity and industriousness of a free Philippine people. For some of the cultural minorities, such as he Yakan of Mindanao* (below left), *the cloth they weave, and particularly the patterns and colours they use, are characteristic of group identity. Conversely, the madly vivid decoration given to the country's jeepneys* (below right), *is a nationwide expression of a uniquely Philippine form of pop art.*

Traditional, pre-European wind instruments include bamboo flutes, played either by mouth or nose, and pan-pipes, a collection of bamboo tubes of different lengths more commonly associated with South America. String instruments include a variety of bamboo lutes and guitar-like instruments, while percussion consists mostly of metal gongs and various forms of bamboo instrument.

In the Islamic areas percussion music is particularly well developed, being very similar to that popularly associated with Indonesia. Gongs figure very prominently, the most important being the *kulintang*, a row of eight gongs of different sizes mounted on a horizontal frame, which is used to play the melody.

The arrival of the Spanish brought a whole new way of expressing music, and with it a completely new set of instruments. Guitars, violins, pianos and even harps found their way into the lives of the Filipinos, and have been firmly fixed there ever since. The American period greatly popularized Western music, and today, although traditional music is cherished and can still be heard in performance, it is inevitably international rock and pop music that dominates popular culture. Filipinos have taken to these styles enthusiastically and skilfully, and there are many talented Filipino singers and bands doing the rounds of hotels and nightclubs right across East and Southeast Asia, almost always generating an enthusiastic response wherever they go.

Filipino literature has a largely colonial history, very little having survived from the pre-Hispanic era, partly because most stories were passed on orally, but due mainly to the thoroughness with which the Spanish destroyed earlier writings, virtually wiping out the native Filipino alphabets. Today, the Roman alphabet is almost universal, with only a couple of tribal groups, the Mangyan of Mindoro for example, still writing stories in their ancient script.

Most of the writings generated during the early part of Spanish rule were religious in nature, but once education became universal in the 19th century much that was written in both Spanish and Tagalog became secular. By the end of the century, such literature became an integral part of the struggle for independence through the writings of José Rizal, M.H. del Pilar and Apolinario Mabini, to name just the most well-known. With the arrival of

Lechon, suckling pig roasted on a spit, is served at streetside stalls all over the country, where it is often accompanied by a rich, thick sauce made from pigs' livers.

A great variety of fruit is available, ranging from the ubiquitous mango (rear of view) and durian (centre), to the less common rambutan (red, front left) and mangosteen (black, front right).

American rule Spanish was replaced by English, and to this day literature is written in 'Taglish', a mixture of English and Tagalog, one of the Filipino languages, revolving around Philippine themes and sentiments. It is produced, almost without exception, for the home market, although some of Rizal's writings have been published in English.

It is a similar story with painting, with almost the whole field owing its modern origins to Spanish control. For much of the colonial period painting depicted religious scenes, executed in the prescribed European style. By the end of Spanish rule this had become so ingrained in Filipino art that local painters could produce images in the Romantic, grand Classical or Impressionist styles to a quality equal to that of the Europeans, a skill that has persisted to this day with modern styles.

As with other art forms, however, there has latterly been a search for Filipino identity in painting, leading to the adoption of local themes, from the revolution to idealized rural genre images to social comment. Pop art finds its most common expression in the imaginative and spectacularly garish decoration that is applied to the country's jeepneys, the elongated jeeps that provide one of the main forms of public transport across the islands.

In the field of handicrafts, growing tourism, both domestic and international, has created a new market for items that are still in daily use among rural peoples, especially the cultural minorities. This includes a wide range of basketry products, from bags and rice containers to trays and floor mats. Woven cloth is also widely produced: the mountain people of the Cordillera Central produce distinctive, colourful styles, some of which have been adapted for use as wall hangings. In the far south, the T'boli and some of the Moslem groups are known for their beautiful materials, whose colours and intricate patterns closely resemble the *ikats* of Indonesia as well as other Malay Moslem styles. In this same region, the Maranao people produce highly elaborate brass vessels and implements.

Woodcarvings are also widely produced, mostly showing Christian, tribal or Islamic influences. The first usually consist of religious images, whereas the second are tribal artefacts that are often still of great importance. They include, for example, *bulol* carvings, simple human images that are guardian deities used to protect home, farm and rice stores. In the Islamic-influenced areas of the southern islands, some highly elaborate woodcarvings are produced, often stylized curvilinear, almost abstract, images.

Wooden furniture, sculptures and artefacts such as rocking horses and chests are also produced in large numbers for the tourist and export markets; these can sometimes be antiqued or distressed to suggest great age and wear.

FOOD AND DRINK

Like so many other aspects of Filipino life, the food and drink of the country show an interesting mixture of influences, mainly Malay, Chinese, Spanish and American. As with most of Asia, rice is the main staple, but unlike many of the Philippines' neighbours, spices beyond garlic and pepper are virtually unheard of. This is somewhat surprising, considering the country's proximity to the old Spice Islands – today's Indonesian Moluccas – which the medieval traders of Europe went to such enormous lengths to reach. The result is a cuisine in which the taste of a meal is usually that of its main ingredient, fish or meat, which comes as a relief to many visitors from the West but may seem a little bland to those used to the spicier flavours of other South and South-east Asian countries.

Most dishes considered to be native Filipino usually consist of rice with some kind of meat, such as fish or chicken, which may or may not come with a sauce. Unsurprisingly, Seafood figures prominently throughout the islands: grouper, tuna, milkfish, squid, crab and prawn are among the most popular dishes.

Standard Filipino dishes include *inihaw na lapu-lapu*, grilled grouper with soy sauce, garlic, salt and pepper, *sinigang*, a sour soup usually containing either fish or chicken and vegetables, and *kare-kare*, a stew of oxtail, beef and vegetables. One of the most commonly encountered national dishes is *adobo*, which is made from squid, pork or chicken cooked in salt, pepper, vinegar and garlic. Although it is considered to be a classically Filipino dish, it actually has Spanish origins.

The Chinese contribution to Philippine cuisine is enormous. Virtually the only alternative to rice lies in various noodle dishes, all of Chinese origin, such as *pancit Canton*, *pancit guisado* and *bihon*. The first two of these consist of fried noodles, round in the case of the former, flat for the latter, while the last is rice vermicelli. All three are usually served with a mixture of meat and vegetables. Other noodle dishes include noodle soups, known as *mami*, which are served with meat or various kinds of dumplings. Standard Filipino dishes can be rather short on vegetables, so often the only way of obtaining them is to order Chinese, such as the *pancit* dishes, or by ordering *chop suey*, mixed fried vegetables, which is a standard in many restaurants.

When it comes to snacks, the Chinese influence seems to be even stronger, with such foods as *siopao*, an enormous

The display at this festival-time streetside stall clearly indicates the range of influences on modern-day Philippine food, from Chinese, through Spanish to American styles.

steamed bun usually stuffed with either chicken or pork, and *lumpia*, huge spring rolls. However, one popular snack that is almost certainly Filipino in origin is *balut*, a boiled duck egg containing an almost fully formed chick, which is widely available from streetside vendors.

Refrigeration is a relatively recent development, so fish are often preserved by smoking, drying or salting before being sold.

As with many Asian countries, American fast food is popular, though the extreme to which that popularity has grown in the Philippines is quite astonishing. Even the smallest towns seem to host at least one outlet, and in the main cities some streets appear to be lined with everything the USA has to offer, from McDonalds, Wendy's and Burger King, through Shakey's Pizza and Pizza Hut, to Dunkin' Donuts and Mr Donut – hamburgers, pizzas and doughnuts are definitely a significant component of modern Philippine cuisine.

Fruit markets are always well stocked with apples, oranges and bananas, and also a wide selection of tropical fruits. Mango and kalamansi, the latter a small lemon-like fruit that is commonly squeezed into main dishes and in drinks, are virtually ubiquitous, available across the entire country.

Other common fruits, though perhaps not quite so widespread, include durian and papaya. While the latter is now quite well known around the world for its beautifully sweet, creamy orange-coloured flesh, the former, known to its adherents as the 'king of fruits', is less familiar to those outside South-east Asia. It is a large fruit with a thick spiny shell, which has the most appalling smell but an extremely rich, sweet taste. It is usually loved or hated. In the Philippines it is grown extensively around Davao, in the south of Mindanao, earning the city the title Durian Capital of the Philippines; when the fruit is in season, its less than pleasant aroma seems to permeate across the entire city!

Sadly, due to the difficulties of distribution, other fruits are often available only in or near the areas where they are cultivated. This applies even to Manila, and affects such fruits as rambutan, *mangostan* (mangosteen), *lanzones* (lanson), *atis* (custard apple) and *langka* (jackfruit).

Strangely enough, coconuts are not as easily available as might be assumed from their importance to the economy. With such a versatile and valuable commodity, its delicious flesh and milk are almost side products, ensuring that the nuts only readily reach the market in tourist areas. In general, the locals get to eat and drink them just whenever they feel like it, without having to buy them from a shop.

When it comes to non-alcoholic drinks, coffee is king. According to some claims the Philippines is one of the world's top ten coffee consumers, with just about all of it produced domestically. However, the visitor will rarely see large coffee plantations, the reason being that many areas that are given over to the crop are relatively small buffer zones on the margins of the forests. The vast majority of the crop goes to make instant coffee, available in supermarkets and village stores alike. Only in a few areas is ground coffee, usually called 'native coffee', available.

For alcoholic drinks the name San Miguel, or 'San Mig' as it is universally known, is virtually synonymous with beer. Despite the Spanish name, this is a Filipino company, churning out beer locally, and making it cheaper to buy than a bottle of water! San Miguel is an integral part of Philippine life, as ubiquitous as the swaying palm trees.

Other alcoholic drinks are those fermented from local crops, such as *tapey*, a wine made from rice, *basi*, a rum distilled from sugar cane, and *tuba*, palm wine from the crown of the coconut palm. The last is also distilled to produce *lambanog*. Filipino whisky, brandy and gin are also produced for local consumption.

THE REGIONS

The Philippines' 7107 islands, divided into 77 provinces, show an enormous diversity in both their people and landscape. From the rugged cliffs and Ivatan people of the

In many rural areas, jeepneys are the only form of public transport. On the Batanes Islands, they wend their way through the rocky hillsides that characterize the northernmost part of the country.

Batanes Islands, the country's northernmost province, through the sophisticated urbanites in Manila, to the coral islands and the Moslems of Tawi-Tawi in the far south, this is a land of extraordinary contrast and variety. The following gazetteer gives an overview of what the visitor can expect to find across the country.

COASTS AND ISLANDS OF NORTH-WEST LUZON

This region encompasses the coastal provinces of La Union, Ilocos Sur and Ilocos Norte, as well as two island groups, the Babuyan and Batanes Islands. The last of these lie in the Luzon Strait that separates the Philippines from Taiwan, and

though remote and often difficult to reach, are known for their friendly people, the Ivatans, as well as the landscape's great beauty, with sheer cliffs alternating with wide, rocky beaches.

The Ilocos region consists of a wide coastal plain bordered to the east by rugged mountains that rise up towards the Cordillera Central, the backbone of northern Luzon. The coastal area is intensely agricultural, growing mainly rice, corn (maize) and tobacco. There are two cities, Laoag and Vigan, the latter the site of the country's best preserved Spanish town. Spain's fourth Philippine settlement, it was established in 1572, and today a large section of Vigan consists of a grid of streets lined with Castilian houses, as well as a number of elegant villas.

To the south lies La Union province, rather similar to Ilocos, and known for the popular beaches that lie close to the provincial capital, San Fernando, built on seven hills.

South of the city is a well-developed beach area, the sands lined with a number of pleasant resorts, while to the north is an enormous stretch of sand that remains almost untouched by development. This has become popular as one of the very few good surfing sites on Luzon's west coast.

NORTH-EAST LUZON

This area is dominated by the Sierra Madre Mountains, which run along much of Luzon's Pacific coast. The coastline remains extremely remote, partly because there are no roads that cross the mountains from the inland lowlands. What access there is to this region must be made solely by aircraft or a very long boat journey.

Such remoteness has ensured that this is one of the few parts of Luzon in which lowland tropical rainforest has survived; its importance has been recognized in that part of it is now included in one of the country's most important, and largest, protected areas. Philippine Eagles have been sighted here, the only place in Luzon where they are known to exist. There are also a number of tribal groups living in these mountains, some of whom still follow traditional practices.

Inland lies the Cagayan Valley, sandwiched between the Sierra Madre and the Cordillera Central. This fertile region, drained by the Cagayan River, the Philippines' longest river, was colonized by migrants from central Luzon only in this century, and it remains lightly populated and largely undiscovered by tourists.

THE MOUNTAINS OF NORTHERN LUZON

The main inland areas of northern Luzon consist of a large mountain range known as the Cordillera Central. This is the homeland for a wide range of cultural minorities, the best known of whom are probably the Ifugao, who built and still farm the mighty rice terraces around Banaue. Traditionally, these people have strongly resisted any form of outside control, and to this day there remains a Cordillera independence movement.

Manila's busy port is both the capital's gateway to the wider world and the terminus for ferry services that serve many of the country's 7000 islands.

The natural vegetation for these high mountains is mostly pine forests, consisting largely of Benguet pine, a species unique to the area. In many of the accessible areas, however, this forest has been cleared to make way for farms that produce most of the Philippines' temperate vegetables, such as tomatoes, cabbages and potatoes. The market in the region's main city, Baguio, is always crammed with produce of this kind.

The Cordillera Central is Luzon's main tourist area, at least to some degree because of the pleasantly cool climate found there. With pine forests and chilly nights it is easy to forget that this is a tropical country, though a sudden reminder awaits anyone returning to the heat and humidity of the lowlands.

CENTRAL LUZON

This is the Philippine heartland, the most densely populated part of the country and the site of Manila, the national capital. The main part of this region consists of an extensive plain that is both intensely agricultural and has many towns. It is bordered to the east by the Sierra Madre Mountains and to the west by the Zambales Mountains, the latter the site of Mount Pinatubo. In the north the lowlands are partially enclosed by the Cordillera Central, but they also border the Lingayen Gulf, where can be found the Hundred Islands, a popular cluster of offshore islets. The southern edge of the lowlands is

In the mountains of the Cordillera Central, many of the pine forests have been cleared and the hillsides terraced for the production of rice and vegetables.

marked by the sprawling mass of Manila, by far the country's largest city and the major industrial region.

Until 1992 the USA had its two largest overseas military bases at Subic Bay Naval Base, near Olongapo, and Clark Air Force Base, near Angeles. Both played major roles in the Vietnam War and Cold War years, but were seriously damaged by the eruption of Mount Pinatubo: Clark was virtually destroyed by the fallout of ash from the volcano. The Americans finally pulled out after the Philippine Congress decided not to renew the leases on any of their bases in the country.

CALABARZON

Consisting of the provinces of Cavite, Laguna, Batangas, Rizal and Quezon, this is the region that lies immediately south and east of Manila. The dominant features here are Laguna de Bay, the country's largest lake, and Lake Taal, a massive volcanic crater that is the site of Taal Island, one of the Philippines' smallest yet most dangerously active volcanoes.

A densely populated area, Laguna de Bay is ringed by towns and covered with fish farms, to the extent that there are now serious pollution concerns. The Taal

The country's largest lake, Laguna de Bay, lies just south of Manila. It is surrounded by a huge population, many of whom rely on the lake for a livelihood, and today many areas of the lake are covered with fish farms.

area, by contrast, is a popular place for weekend breaks from Manila, the high hills that surround the lake offering a reasonably cool climate, especially at night. Close to the southern shores of Laguna de Bay are two more volcanoes, the inactive Makiling, and the active Banahaw. The former is covered with dense rainforest, protected and intensively studied by the nearby campus of the University of the Philippines. The latter is something of a sacred mountain, with many pilgrims climbing to its summit at Easter.

Along the west coast are Manila's nearest beaches, notably Nasugbu and Matabungkay, while to the south, near Batangas, are some well-known diving sites with good coral reefs.

BICOL

The narrow, southernmost projection of Luzon Island, this region consists of the provinces of Sorsogon, Camarines Sur, Albay, Catanduanes, and Camarines Norte. It is a land of rice cultivation: much of the area is flat and low-lying, though there is also some extensive volcanic landscape, the most important being Mount Mayon, the most active volcano in the Philippines. This enormous 2421 metre (7941 feet) volcano sweeps up from sea level to its summit crater in an almost perfect cone that towers over nearby Legaspi.

This city, the region's largest, is constantly under threat from Mayon's erup-

The beautiful resort area of Puerto Galera, on the northern coast of Mindoro, is quite easily reached from Manila, and is a main attraction for visitors and Manila residents. The shoreline at Big La Laguna Beach is always a magnet for children.

tions (the latest was in 1993), though to date these have been relatively small. The only other active volcano in the region is Mount Bulusan, which lies, surrounded by rainforest, close to the southern tip of Luzon. Several inactive volcanoes, including Mounts Iriga, Isarog and Labo, lie further to the north.

What little tourism development there is in this area is geared towards adventure, in particular climbing the volcanoes. The island of Catanduanes is known for its beaches, and particularly for its surfing. A recent development has been the discovery of Whale Sharks off the coast of Sorsogon, which has now resulted in the development of boat trips to watch and perhaps swim with these giant fish.

MINDORO

This mountainous island is divided into two provinces, Oriental and Occidental Mindoro, which cover the island's eastern and western portions respectively. Although it lies very close to Luzon, just south of the Calabarzon region and easily reached from Batangas, this island is a world away from the hustle and bustle of the crowded central regions.

Extremely mountainous and with only a relatively small population (most of it along the coasts), Mindoro remains largely undeveloped and wild. The island is the home of the Mangyan, a tribal people who still follow many traditional practices and have so far resisted outside influences over their lifestyle.

The only part of Mindoro that sees extensive tourism is around the small town and peninsula of Puerto Galera, in the far north. Here, a series of beaches set in a beautiful landscape and with excellent diving over protected coral reefs attracts a steady stream of visitors.

WESTERN VISAYAS

This region consists of the islands of Panay, Negros, Guimaras and the Romblon group. The first three are highly agricultural: Negros is renowned as the centre of Philippine sugar cane production, with over half of its land area given over to the crop. Guimaras's main product is mangoes, whose orchards stretch across large parts of the island. Romblon is known for its marble products, derived from its rich marble deposits.

Panay is a large triangular island divided into four provinces, Iloilo, Capiz, Antique and Aklan, with the largest city, also called Iloilo, located in the south in the province of that name. Today, it is a city of 300,000, with one of the largest ports in the Visayas, sprawling along the banks of the Iloilo River. Most of the island is fairly low-lying, apart from a mountain range that runs along the western half, mostly in Antique province.

Panay's fame outside the Philippines is mostly due to the island of Boracay, which lies off the far northern tip of Panay and

White Beach, Boracay, is famous throughout the world as the quintessential tropical beach. With some of South-east Asia's most spectacular beaches, Boracay is by far the Philippines' number one attraction for visitors from overseas.

The huge, imposing Taoist Temple overlooking the northern hilly suburbs of Cebu City testifies to both the numbers and wealth of the city's ethnic Chinese, many of whom play major roles in the local and national economy.

has become one of the country's best-known tourist attractions. This tiny island – only 7 kilometres (4 miles) in length – is renowned internationally for its stunning white beaches, and for this reason alone attracts tens of thousands of visitors each year from all over the world.

Negros is a rectangular island, divided into two provinces, Negros Oriental and Negros Occidental. The western half of the island consists of a large plain which is given over mainly to sugar cane cultivation, while the eastern half is mountainous, consisting of a chain of volcanoes. Only one of these, Mount Kanlaon, is active, and is also the site of Negros's largest remaining tract of rainforest.

EASTERN VISAYAS

This region consists of the islands of Cebu, Bohol, Masbate, Samar and Leyte, along with a whole host of smaller islands. Cebu City, the capital of the province and island of the same name, is the commercial hub of the entire Visayan region. Economically

the country's second most important city and the site of its largest port, it has been a major trade and cultural centre for at least the past thousand years, and was the site of Spain's first settlement in the Philippines, originally established by Miguel Legaspi in 1565.

Bohol, to the south-east of Cebu, is the site of the Chocolate Hills, a strange landscape of hundreds of small rounded hills, so-called because of their colour at the end of the dry season. Bohol also has a number of excellent beaches, particularly around the small island of Panglao, where there are superb coral reefs. The nearby islet of Balicasag offers some of the best diving in the Philippines, while a little further to the east whales and dolphins are commonly seen.

Masbate and the twin islands of Samar and Leyte, the latter two linked by a bridge, are off the beaten track. Samar and Leyte are thinly populated, and there are still extensive tracts of rainforest that are home to rare flora and fauna.

EASTERN MINDANAO

The eastern half of Mindanao consists of mountain ranges that run roughly north-south through the centre of the island, and another running along the Pacific coast, separated by a lowland drained by the Agusan River. Much of this lowland constitutes one of the largest remaining freshwater swamps in the country, the site of a unique swamp forest that is home to such rare animals as the Philippine Crocodile and Purple Heron.

The central mountain range contains the country's two highest mountains, Mounts Apo and Dulang-Dulang, 2954 metres (9689 feet) and 2938 metres (9637 feet) high respectively. Both are surrounded by rainforest and are known to be strongholds of the Philippine Eagle.

In the south is Davao, the country's second largest city, economically the third most important. Though today enjoying a boom, in the 1980s Davao was a dangerous place, known for its lawlessness, wracked by insurrection and street fighting between rebel and government forces. Peace returned in the early 1990s, with a treaty between the government and the communist New People's Army.

Although these days increasing numbers of hikers are visiting Mount Apo, the most popular destination for visitors in this area is Camiguin Island, a jewel off Mindanao's north coast. Dominated by several volcanoes, including the active Hibok-Hibok, this is a lush island that is populated by immensely friendly people, and ringed by pleasant beaches.

Of increasing importance to the burgeoning tourist industry is Siargao Island, off Mindanao's north-east coast, where imposing waves have made it the Philippines' latest surfing mecca.

WESTERN MINDANAO

Although much of this area is mountainous, the easternmost part consists of the Liguasan Marsh, like the Agusan Marsh a vast and ecologically important swamp. To the north-west lies Lake Lanao, a crater lake in the mountains, that is home to the T'boli people, one of a whole host of cultural minorities living in this region.

From the Lake Lanao area, the mountains of western Mindanao run westwards and then south-west into the Zamboanga peninsula. The area's main city, Zamboanga, lies at the southern tip of this peninsula. Most of the population of western Mindanao is Moslem, and it is here that the new Moslem autonomous region is being established.

Apart from the beach resorts at Dapitan on the north coast, this is generally not recommended as an area for visitors or other outsiders to travel to, since it is in western Mindanao that the two remaining Islamic separatist groups, Abu Sayyaf and the Moro Islamic Liberation Front (MILF), are still active. For all its ecological importance, Liguasan Marsh is the headquarters of the MILF and has been the site of clashes between the separatists and government forces. Abu Sayyaf has conducted sporadic attacks, mainly in the Zamboanga peninsula and on Basilan Island to the south.

SULU ISLANDS
The Sulu Islands consist of a scattered island chain that stretches for nearly 400 kilometres (250 miles) south-west from Zamboanga almost as far as the coast of Borneo, and which is divided into two provinces, Sulu and Tawi-Tawi. The population of the islands is almost entirely Moslem, derived from Moslem Malays and Chinese, as well as some Arabs that either passed through on trading missions or came to settle here from the 13th century onwards.

The central government of the Philippines in Manila has never found it easy to assert its authority here, which is hardly surprising in an area that is both culturally and physically far removed from most of the country. There is a long history of internal conflict between the various peoples, and the islands have at times held a reputation for piracy.

The magnificent sheer limestone cliffs that mark the edge of many of the islands in the Bacuit archipelago make El Nido one of the most striking sites in the remote region of Palawan.

PALAWAN
Often called the final frontier of the Philippines because of its extensive forests and remoteness from the rest of the country, this long ribbon of land, composed of one main island and 1700 smaller ones, is a single province. Although it is currently only lightly populated, there is nevertheless a process of rapid immigration under way from the more crowded parts of the country, making it ever more likely that much of the remaining forest will be cut back in order to satisfy the demand for new residential areas.

The capital of Palawan, Puerto Princesa, was created as recently as 1972, but already has a population of 120,000, mostly people of Visayan origin. Beyond the city limits, road communications to the towns in the south are reasonable, at least as far as Quezon. To the north travel can be more difficult, especially during the rainy season, when the road conditions deteriorate. In many places the quickest way to get around is by boat.

There is little of historical significance in Palawan, with the exception of the Tabon Cave, near the town of Quezon, where human remains dating back 50,000 years have been discovered. The island's main attractions are environmental, in particular St Paul's Underground River, located on the west coast to the north of Puerto Princesa; El Nido, a bay of magnificent rocky islands in the far north; and Calauit Island in the Calamian Islands, where herds of imported African animals roam freely in the natural landscape as part of a wildlife experiment that has been running for over 20 years.

One other part of the Palawan province that has attracted the interest of environmentalists is the Tubbataha Reef National Marine Park, a huge coral reef and islet complex that lies south-east of Puerto Princesa, in the Sulu Sea between Palawan and Mindanao. The future of this beautiful and pristine area now appears to be more secure, having recently been declared a world heritage site by UNESCO.

Apart from its obvious economic importance in providing most of the fish fry that supports the fishing industry in Palawan, the reef is also a marvellous – if extremely isolated – diving site, with a wealth of underwater creatures and some remarkable and unspoilt coral on show to those who make the journey there.

AROUND THE NORTHERN ISLANDS
COASTAL NORTH LUZON

Coastal north Luzon encompasses a diverse region of the Philippines, from the suburbs of Manila in the south to the wild and remote Batanes Islands in the far north. The latter, ringed with rugged cliffs quite unlike anywhere else in the Philippines, and isolated from the outside world for much of the year by storms, are truly a place apart. They are populated by the Ivatan, a unique ethnic group, for whom life consists mainly of subsistence farming and fishing. Electricity and motor transport are new developments, having arrived on the islands only in the last few years. Communications remain poor: telephones are virtually unheard of, there is no regular ferry, and flight services to the mainland are frequently interrupted.

What a contrast this makes with bustling Subic Bay, on the west coast of north Luzon and within easy reach of the capital. A former American naval base and now an important free port and industrial zone, Subic is also quite separate from much of the Philippines, but for entirely different reasons. Here, despite the withdrawal of the American military in 1992, an American-style orderliness and relative wealth are prominent. Subic has one of the country's most important wild environments, with much of the old base area enveloped in a huge expanse of rainforest. This is home to a group of Negrito, or Aeta, tribesmen and to a great array of animal wildlife, from macaques, wild pig and a colony of fruit bats to vast numbers of forest birds, many of them quite used to humans.

East of Subic stands Mount Pinatubo, a volcano infamous for its massive 1991 eruption, which killed hundreds of people and devastated two of the USA's biggest overseas military bases – Clark Field Air Force Base and Subic Bay. Today, the huge areas buried under ash still resemble a grey moonscape, although some are now being colonized by grasses. The volcano itself seems quiet for the moment, but thousands of people are endangered every rainy season by the unstable lahar that frequently pours down into the lowlands under the weight of heavy rain. During the dry season, however, it is possible for visitors to go hiking on the mountain's slopes or hire an airplane to get a bird's-eye view of the volcano and its enormous crater.

To the north of Subic lie the Hundred Islands, an attractive collection of limestone islets, while beyond here are north Luzon's main beaches, clustered around the city of San Fernando. Further north is Vigan, a beautifully preserved town that is one of the Philippines' most important Spanish legacies.

The Batanes Islands mark the most
northerly point of the Philippines, lying
halfway between the northernmost tip of
the Philippine mainland and Taiwan. In this,
the most isolated part of the country, life
remains simple. Only three of the islands,
Batan, Sabtang and Itbayat, are inhabited,
almost all the 15,000 people belonging to
the Ivatan cultural minority. Traditional
island houses consist of thatch-roofed stone
structures (above left), solidly built to resist
the area's fierce storms. Nakanmuan
(opposite, above), on the western shore of
Sabtang and surrounded by rugged
scenery, is a typical village.

Unlike the bancas, the outriggers typical of
most of the Philippines, boats in the Batanes
are monohulls made from solid planks of
local timber (left). These boats are designed
both to handle rough seas and, with few
harbours on the islands, to be small enough
to be pulled high up onto the stony beaches,
as at the tiny village of San Joaquin, on
Batan (opposite, below). Rough seas are
prevalent throughout much of the year, so
fishing is a sideline occupation and the
catch is small. What fish is caught is usually
preserved by drying (above).

PREVIOUS PAGES
Page 42: The imposing church in the capital
town of Batan, Basco, is one of the few
reminders of the Spanish presence left.
Page 43: A profusion of flowers surrounds
an old Batanes house.

Established as the capital of the far north in 1572 by Juan de Salcedo, Vigan is today the Philippines' best preserved Spanish city, An entire section of Vigan consists of streets lined with old Spanish houses (above), *from which motor transport has been banned. Here, the horse-drawn* calesa *remains the main means of getting around, while in the modern part of the city, public transport consists of decorated motorised tricycles (right). The old district also contains a number of elegant Spanish villas, some of which, including the Villa Angela (opposite, above), are now hotels. These still provide a glimpse of the elegant life of their colonial owners, with the décor showing an eclectic mix of Spanish, Chinese and Malay influences (opposite, below left). A range of arts and crafts flourishes in Vigan, including the production of* burnay *pots* (opposite, below right), *huge storage jars which have been produced in the city for hundreds of years.*

The north of the Philippines is not as well known for its beaches as some of the more southerly islands, but one popular beach area lies around San Fernando, the capital of La Union province, south of Vigan. There is a good surfing beach to the north of the city at San Juan but the most popular area lies a few kilometres to the south, at the village of Bauang. Here, a long stretch of sand is lapped by calm seas (opposite, above), and many attractive hotels have been established (opposite, below), mostly catering for Filipinos and expatriates seeking respite from the urban bustle. Despite being 150 kilometres (93 miles) north of Manila, Bauang is easily accessible from the capital, and large numbers of Manila residents visit the village at the weekends, using the beach and hotels not only for rest and relaxation but also for parties and wedding receptions.

For visitors to the northern beaches who like being active, there are many boats available for hire (left), for sightseeing tours and fishing expeditions.

On the other side of the Lingayen Gulf from the beaches of San Fernando lies a cluster of small coralline limestone islands known as the Hundred Islands. Protected as a national recreation area administered by the Philippine Tourism Authority, this is a popular place for visitors, with a well-regulated system of outrigger boat hire (opposite, below) for island visits and tours that operate out of the nearby mainland village of Lucap. Most of the islands consist of vertical cliffs of limestone, topped by scrubby forest, on which it is impossible to land. Indeed, many have been undercut by the sea; as a result, the smallest islets form attractive 'tables' that hang above the surrounding shallow waters (left).

On the other side of the Lingayen Gulf from the beaches of San Fernando lies a cluster of small coralline limestone islands known as the Hundred Islands. Protected as a national recreation area administered by the Philippine Tourism Authority, this is a popular place for visitors, with a well-regulated system of outrigger boat hire (opposite, below) for island visits and tours that operate out of the nearby mainland village of Lucap. Most of the islands consist of vertical cliffs of limestone, topped by scrubby forest, on which it is impossible to land. Indeed, many have been undercut by the sea; as a result, the smallest islets form attractive 'tables' that hang above the surrounding shallow waters (left).

South of the Hundred Islands along the north Luzon coast, the former naval base of Subic Bay is now a major free port and industrial zone. With its fine bay and dense rainforest, Subic is also being developed as a recreational area, with a new yacht club on the bayside (below left) and a number of grand hotels. In contrast, the rainforest presents ideal opportunities for ecotourism; among the many species to be found there a large colony of fruit bats (left) attracts many visitors. Subic's indigenous Aeta tribesmen (above) trained American GIs in jungle survival during the Vietnam War. They now demonstrate their jungle skills to others: deep in the forest a member of Subic's Jungle Environmental Survival Training Center shows how to make eating utensils out of bamboo (opposite, below right).

One of the last remaining dipterocarp lowland rainforests in Luzon, characterized by trees with extremely tall, straight trunks (opposite, above right), is found at Subic Bay. In some areas the forest comes right down to the shore and merges with the mangroves (opposite, above left). The forest is home to a wide range of wildlife, including many species of birds unique to the Philippines; one of the rarest, and most endangered, is the Luzon Bleeding-Heart Pigeon (opposite, below left).

North-east of Subic Bay lies Mount Pinatubo, whose eruption in June 1991 was one of the largest and most dramatic volcanic explosions of the 20th century. Although no lava was produced, huge quantities of ash were thrown into the atmosphere, turning day into night as far away as Manila, 80 kilometres (50 miles) to the south-east, and affecting weather patterns around the world. The force of the explosion blew off the mountain's summit, reducing its height from 1700 to 1400 metres (5577 to 4593 feet) and creating a massive new crater, now filled by a vivid blue lake (left).

Heavy rain, caused by a typhoon that swept through the region shortly after the eruption finished, brought enormous quantities of ash, or lahar, pouring down the mountain (above), and led to massive devastation around two towns on the mountain's south-eastern side, Angeles and San Fernando in Pampanga province. When

the deluge of lahar finally came to a standstill, entire towns and villages had been buried and hundreds of people killed. Lahars also poured down Pinatubo's western slopes into Zambales province and down to the coast. Damage was severe, and a number of enormous lahar-choked river estuaries were created, cutting road communications along the coast for quite some time (above).

The Mount Pinatubo region now draws a few adventurous visitors in the dry season, who hike through the dramatic landscape, or survey the scene from light aircraft.

Today, still threatened by lahars during each rainy season, a half-buried church – where the doorway was once the second floor window – serves as a reminder of the devastation in Pampanga province (right).

55

THROUGH THE
HIGHLAND MOUNTAINS
THE NORTH LUZON INTERIOR

The mountains of northern Luzon, known as the Cordillera Central, are without doubt the main attraction for visitors coming to the northern half of the Philippines. The scenery is spectacular, with rugged mountain chains dissected by deep, cavernous valleys, and pine forests alternating with terraced fields and villages. The region is inhabited by

some of the country's most accessible cultural minorities, among them the Ifugao, Bontoc and Kalinga. An added bonus is the cool weather. With many of the towns at an altitude of 1400–1500 metres (4593–4920 feet), temperatures are rarely uncomfortably high and nights are wonderfully cool, complete with brilliantly starlit skies.

The largest city in the Cordillera is Baguio, sprawling across steep, rolling hills nearly 1500 metres (4920 feet) above sea level. The Philippines' summer capital during American rule, Baguio is the first stop for many people starting a tour of the mountains or in search of respite from the lowland heat. Although the downtown area is as crowded and noisy as any Filipino city, the fringes of the city, especially to the east where the Botanical Garden and Club John Hay can be found, are filled with pine trees, giving the feeling of a town scattered through the forest. Club John Hay, formerly an American military leisure club, is particularly beautiful, with rolling parkland and fine mountain views.

On leaving Baguio, most visitors travel northwards along the steep, rough Halsema Road towards Bontoc, the capital of Mountain province. Climbing to 2200 metres (7217 feet), the highest point of any road in the Philippines, the Halsema offers incredible all-round mountain views and passes through a number of townships.

To the west, high in the mountains above Bontoc, is Sagada, an isolated village lost in a beautiful pine forest, the perfect mountain retreat; cool and quiet, the air is stunningly clean and scented by the perfume of thousands of pine trees. Hiking trails radiate out into the mountains from here, leading to summits, waterfalls and caves. One unusual aspect of Sagada is the local custom of burying the dead in nearby caves, or even in coffins attached to cliffs. Echo Valley, a narrow limestone gorge close to Sagada, is one location where these hanging coffins can be found.

To the south-east of Bontoc is the small town of Banaue, the centre of the Ifugao cultural minority's homeland and the site of their stupendous rice terraces. Created over 2000 years ago, the terraces, still used for rice cultivation, climb high up the mountainsides. Banaue is a good base from which to explore the surrounding mountains, to visit remote Ifugao villages and to discover something of the culture of this unique ethnic group.

The North Luzon region is well known for its handicrafts, including colourful textiles; one of the best places for the visitor to see the textiles being woven is at the Easter School of Weaving in Baguio (left). This mountain town is sometimes known as the 'city of Pines': at the Club John Hay, pine forests predominate in a vast expanse of green (opposite, above). In the surrounding mountains, some of the most precipitous valleys are crossed by cable suspension bridges, making it possible to get around difficult terrain (below right). Rural life around Baguio is still dependent on nature's bounty; here a mountain stream provides the opportunity for an entire community to take a bath (below left).

PREVIOUS PAGES
Page 56: *The ancient rice terraces of the Ifugao at Banaue.*
Page 57: *Traditional baskets are still woven and used by the Ibaloi people around Baguio.*

The glorious pine forests and lofty mountains of the Cordillera Central (top), here looking towards Mount Pulag, at 2930 metres (9612 feet) the highest mountain on Luzon, are within easy reach of Baguio. Near the town, Mines View Park draws visitors to admire its spectacular mountain view and perhaps to sample barbecued corn and squid at its snack stalls (left). Many trips to the mountains start at Baguio; here a young boy, ready with a smile (above), waits for his jeepney to set off.

Lake Ambuklao (opposite), a large reservoir, lies east of Baguio in the Cordillera Central. Seen here in the dry season, the landscape is parched and the lake's water levels are reduced. The challenge of providing water to cities throughout the year means that watershed management is becoming a crucial issue.

Close to the township of Ambangeg, many vegetable farms are found on the terraced lower slopes of Mount Pulag (above). Although these are not as spectacular as the mighty Banaue rice terraces for which the mountains of the Cordillera Central are famed, many of the hills in this area are terraced in a relatively simple way to enable greater vegetable production on the steep slopes. It is on such farms that most of the Philippines' temperate vegetables are produced.

An overwhelming majority of Filipinos practise Catholicism, but many of the inhabitants of the Cordillera Central belong to non-Christian, animist cultural minorities, including the Kalinga, Kankaney, Ifugao, Bontoc, Isneg, Kalanguya, Balangao and Ibaloi. For large numbers of these peoples, the spirit world is still all-important in their daily lives, and rituals such as feasting, fasting, shamanism, dancing and sacrifices are common. Even where the practice of Catholicism is predominant, it is often inextricably mixed with elements of the local religions. Carved deity figures, such as Kabunyian, regarded as the creator of the other gods, help to protect homes, food stores and crops in the field from attack and destruction. These striking wooden images, such as this one carved on a gatepost high up on Mount Pulag (left), an area mainly inhabited by the Ibaloi and Kalanguya minorities, are typical and widespread in the region.

At an altitude of 1400 metres (4593 feet), the village of Sagada (right) is one of the most beautiful places in the Cordillera mountains. Its refreshingly cool climate makes for a wonderful break from the sticky heat of the lowlands, while the clean, fresh air is further enhanced by the fragrant pine forest in which the village stands. Quite difficult to reach in the mountains above Bontoc, it remains a quiet backwater, which nevertheless has a number of simple guesthouses that cater for adventurous visitors.

Sagada is also known for its local burial custom of placing the coffins of the dead either inside certain nearby caves or hung on a prominent cliff face. Many of the more accessible coffins are quite recent; the chair, to which the deceased is strapped during part of the mourning period, may also be placed at the final burial site (below left). Guided walks through the dramatic limestone formations in the caves (below right) are popular with visitors.

Banaue is famed for its magnificent ancient rice terraces, constructed some 2000 years ago by the ancestors of the Ifugao people who farm there to this day. Some of the largest and most spectacular terraces lie around the village of Batad (opposite), 18 kilometres (11 miles) from Banaue and a two-hour hike from the nearest road. The fine agricultural mountain scenery repays the effort required to reach this village. Here, as in other such areas, the only way to get around is along narrow footpaths that follow the sometimes precipitous terrace edges (top). With years of practice, even the older Ifugao are able to negotiate these paths with agility, whereas newly arrived visitors often find them a giddying, even unnerving, experience.

Traditional costume is usually seen only on the older Ifugao (above left and right), and is on show more often during festivals. The headdress, adorned with textiles, shells, cock feathers and even animal skulls, is an important indication of the wearer's status.

The main inhabitants of Ifugao province in the mountains of the Cordillera Central are the Ifugao people, whose ancestors built the mighty rice terraces that still cover so many of the mountainsides in the area around Banaue (left). On such steep hillsides often the only way to get around, for instance to reach school, is to follow paths that have been made along the edges of the rice terraces (opposite, above).

An independent-minded people who fiercely resisted both Spanish and American control, the Ifugao still maintain many of their traditional customs. Although their wooden, stilted houses are today often roofed with metal, in more remote areas bamboo slats overlayed with thatch are still commonly used (opposite, above right). Traditional costume is rarely worn now, except for the benefit of visitors (right and opposite, below right) and at festival time and during the preparation of feasts (opposite, above left).

Ifugao rites, such as the cañao, often involve the ritual slaughter of water buffalo, pigs and chickens, the skulls of the first two and the hutches of the last later being hung up on the walls of the owner's house (above) – the more skulls, the greater the status.

THE HEART OF THE NATION
MANILA, SOUTH LUZON AND MINDORO

Lying on the mouth of the Pasig River in the central part of Luzon, Manila, the capital of the Philippines, is the country's largest city by far. With a population of over 10 million, it is home to over one-third of the Philippines' entire urban population. It is the country's seat of government, its economic powerhouse and the

focus for much of its wealth, as well as being a sophisticated and cosmopolitan international centre.

This vast metropolis, created in the 1970s by the merger of eight cities and nine towns, consists of Manila itself and Metro Manila. Sitting on the shore of Manila Bay, the former officially consists of the older districts, such as Intramuros, Ermita, Malate, Paco and Binondo, all of which are clustered around the lower reaches of the Pasig River. Beyond them lies Metro Manila, a massive conurbation, the best-known areas of which are Pasay to the south, Makati to the southeast and Mandaluyong to the east. The latter two districts are the most internationally oriented of the city, with Makati firmly established as the hub of business and commerce in the Philippines.

Immediately south of Manila lies Calabarzon, a region of Luzon that contains two lakes, hot springs, volcanoes, beach resorts and a famous waterfall. The southern edge of Metro Manila reaches to the northern shore of Laguna de Bay, the

country's largest lake; on its southern shore is Los Baños, renowned for its hot springs, its prestigious University of the Philippines and Mount Makiling, a dormant volcano. Round the lake to the east is Pagsanjan, with a renowned waterfall which can be reached only by a raft trip on a fast-flowing river. Lake Taal, a huge flooded caldera and home to Taal Island, a highly active volcano, lies further to the south. The area around the lake, with its stunning views and cool mountain air, is a popular destination for Manila residents and visitors.

Excellent diving – some of the best in the country – is to be had in the warm tropical waters between the far south of the Calabarzon region and northern Mindanao. Here, dive resorts such as Anilao, near Batangas, and Puerto Galera, on Mindoro's northern coast, provide first-rate facilities for divers to explore the colourful coral reefs. Puerto Galera, with beautiful beaches and a lovely natural harbour, is deservedly popular; its well protected reefs offer spectacular underwater experiences.

Luzon's southernmost region, known as Bicol, is an agricultural land. The largest city here is Legaspi, famous for its position at the foot of the awesome Mount Mayon, the country's most active volcano. Another, Mount Bulusan, lies close to Luzon's southern tip and is the site of one of Bicol's last remaining tracts of rainforest.

Close to the Rizal Monument in central Manila are a number of murals celebrating the Filipino people. One shows an elongated jeepney (top left) *driven by national hero José Rizal. His passengers are a happy, sharing, studious and industrious people, who live in a green and productive land. In this huge city, however, the streets are filled with non-stop life and bustle in a hectic mix of old and new, of wealth and poverty. Jeepneys and McDonald's* (middle left), *both popular, crowded and economical, are seen on almost every Manila street, while roadside shacks* (below right) *spring up to supply simple, inexpensive meals to the workers who build the high-rise apartment blocks in exclusive areas. Many children grow up playing in the street* (below left), *even around the former palace of Ferdinand and Imelda Marcos.*

PREVIOUS PAGES

Page 68: *Epifanio de los Santos Avenue, known as EDSA, is one of Manila's busiest main arteries. As it passes through Guadalupe, on the edge of Mandaluyong City, advertising signs vie for space at the side of the road.*

Page 69: *Bottles filled with folk remedies are widely available, especially in the markets around Quiapo Church; many Filipinos believe in the effectiveness of the remedies.*

To the north of the Pasig River in the Binondo district of Manila, many of the streets are filled with atmospheric markets selling everything from folk medicines, vegetables, meat and fish to clothes and household goods (right). This area is often known as Chinatown as it has been the focus for many Chinese businesses since the 17th century.

South of the Pasig River lies Intramuros, originally a Malay settlement and then the old walled city that was the capital of the Philippines in Spanish times. The Spanish took control in 1571, initially constructing a wooden settlement but soon rebuilding and fortifying it with stone. Intramuros has been badly damaged a number of times, most recently at the end of World War II, but many parts have survived. A number of fine buildings, as well as attractive courtyards that provide a cool retreat from the heat of the sun (right), and evocative street names (above) still bear witness to the Spanish colonial heritage.

Filipinos love festivals and there is certainly no shortage of them throughout the country, from ancient rites, through religious processions, to parades of national pride. The main example of the latter is Independence Day, an annual holiday on 12 June, the anniversary of the Philippine Declaration of Independence, issued in 1898. The day is marked in Manila by a large parade on the edge of Rizal Park. People from all walks of Philippine life take part in the procession, including representatives of some of the country's cultural minorities, who have the opportunity to display their group identities (above right). The spectacle continues throughout the afternoon and is watched by large crowds, a lucky few of whom escape the sun and heat by securing seats in the covered stadium (above left).

The Independence Day parade is mostly a military show. The procession includes soldiers dressed in ceremonial uniform (left), based on Spanish dress uniforms of the 19th century, and modern military units who parade in jungle combat gear.

One of Manila's largest religious festivals is the Festival of the Black Nazarene, held annually on 9 January. There are many Black Nazarene statues of Christ in the Philippines, but the most important is kept at Quiapo Church in the north of Manila. This example is believed to have been made by an Aztec in Mexico and to have been brought to Manila in the 17th century. On the day of the festival the statue is paraded through the streets of Quiapo, an event that attracts huge crowds (right).

To touch any part of the statue, its palanquin, or even the ropes used to pull it, is considered to bring absolution of all sins. Not surprisingly, the Festival becomes highly charged as thousands struggle to reach the statue. Those who do frequently climb over and across the heads of others, and then, with their mission completed, dive off the palanquin into the crowd. From start to finish the statue's progress is extremely slow, the throng making it almost impossible for the procession to leave the church (below). Even to cross the church-front plaza and enter the first street can take a couple of hours.

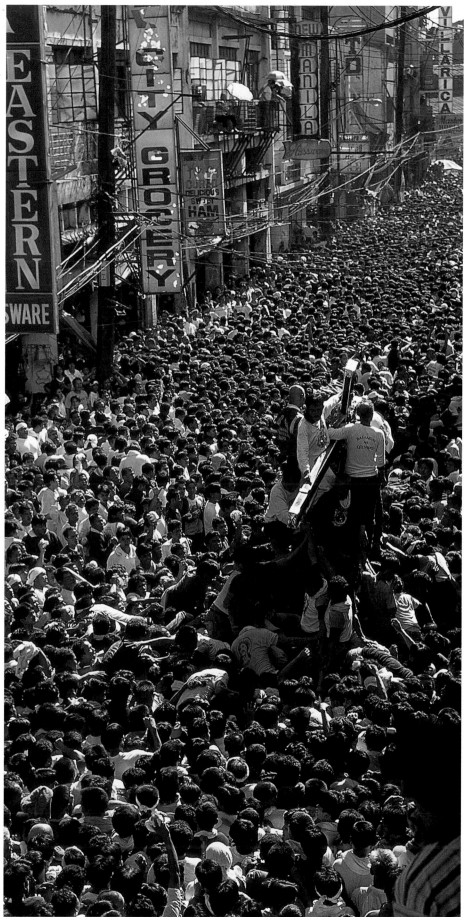

Bustling by day and just as lively at night, each of Metro Manila's metropolitan areas has its own characteristics. Makati (left) is the economic hub of the country, the area in which most international corporations have their Philippine headquarters. Its glittering night-time skyline is an indication of growing corporate confidence. Much of the wealth generated by trade passes through the city's port (top), which lies to both the north and south of the mouth of the Pasig River. Shipping here provides not only freight services to destinations throughout Asia, but also essential ferry services to all parts of the archipelago.

Manila is renowned for its nightlife, with superb restaurants and nightclubs and a wide variety of cultural entertainments from all over South-east Asia. On the open-air stage at Rizal Park, a performance of Filipino folk dancing (above) is a dazzling blend of colourful costumes, sinuous movements and traditional music.

75

Covering 927 square kilometres (356 square miles), Laguna de Bay is the Philippines' largest lake and one of its most scenic. Just south of Manila, it is popular with city residents who come to visit the hot springs and waterfalls near its shores. While single fishermen still go after their catch with a simple rod and net (left), a large proportion of the lake is covered with picturesque fish farms built on stilts (above), one cause of the concern for the lake's condition.

Close to the lakeside town of Los Baños is the Philippine Raptor Center, where a number of Philippine birds of prey are kept for study. One of the main stars is Leila, a Crested Serpent-Eagle (below right), *who is so tame that she can be picked up by complete strangers. Other birds at the Center include* Philippine Hawk-Eagles (top right), *which are are unique to the country. Though widely spread they are rare and now endangered by the loss of their forest habitat.*

The University of the Philippines is one of the country's most prestigious centres of higher education. The Los Baños campus (middle right) *is laid out on a site filled with tree specimens from around South-east Asia, which gradually merge with the dense rainforest covering Mount Makiling behind.*

Mount Makiling lies just to the south of Laguna de Bay. Although it occupies only a few thousand hectares, its forest is one of the best preserved in the country. It is also the site of the Philippines' first national park, created in 1911 soon after the Los Baños campus of the University of the Philippines was established on its northern edge. Much of the forest consists of dense stands of dipterocarp trees (opposite) and tangles of rattans and lianas (above right). Because it has been well protected, wildlife is common and can usually be approached. One of the best known birds found here is the Green Imperial Pigeon (left).

At the foot of Mount Makiling lie the hot springs of Los Baños. On its middle slopes is an area called 'Mudspring', literally a series of pools filled with boiling mud (above left). Although Mount Makiling is officially dormant, the springs and mud pools are reminders that there is still volcanic activity here.

To the south-west of Laguna de Bay lies Lake Taal, a massive volcanic caldera. The lake was at one time an inlet from the sea, but a series of eruptions in the 18th century sealed it off. Today, large numbers of fish farms (above) are found on the lake and villages line its shore. Many of the people of the villages can trace their ancestry back to the chieftains who fled Borneo in the 13th century and settled around Lake Taal; as well as fishing, they established rice cultivation, weaving and fine embroidery in the area, all of which their descendants continue to practice to this day.

In the centre of Lake Taal is Taal Island (right), one of the country's smallest but most active volcanoes. The first recorded eruption was in 1572, and there have been over 30 others since then; the last took place in 1977. The volcanic soils here are rich and the surrounding waters productive, but the very presence of the island makes for a precarious existence for the fish farmers who live and work in its shadow.

The warm waters and coral reefs of the Philippines are a paradise for divers, not least for the diversity of marine life they harbour. The best-known diving takes place around Anilao, near the tip of the Calumpan Peninsula, south of Lake Taal. Overlooking the sheltered waters of Balayan Bay, west of the port of Batangas, Anilao is a weekend mecca for Manila-based divers. Many of the dives along the peninsula are reached by banca, while others, further offshore, are reached by 'safari' dive boats (above).

The Anilao region is known for its profusion of colourful reef life and corals. Brilliantly patterned fish and invertebrates, including sea cucumbers, nudibranchs, anemones and sponges, abound. Sea fans (opposite, below) are particularly common, as are feather stars (right). Among other common corals are the Tubbastrea cup corals (above right). When currents are slack these resemble clusters of simple cups, but when the tide starts to run, a mass of golden yellow tentacles protrude. Here, a group of soldierfish patrols the reef, gliding past the cup corals and black hard corals.

Just south of Anilao, and only a ferry ride across the water from Batangas on the Luzon mainland, is Puerto Galera, situated on the northernmost tip of Mindoro. A peninsula and a group of islands together create a stunningly beautiful, enclosed natural harbour (above), in which sits the delightful little town of Puerto Galera (below left). Known as the 'pearl of Mindoro', Puerto Galera has been used as a harbour since the 10th century. During the Spanish period, each year's newly built Manila Galleon would prepare for its cross-Pacific voyage here, giving rise to the town's name 'Puerto Galera', meaning 'port of galleons'.

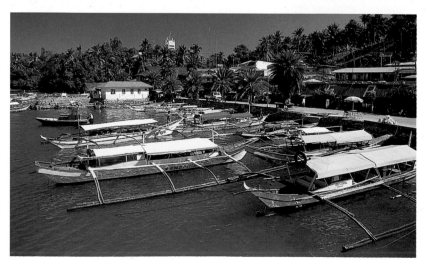

The many fine beaches in the Puerto Galera area are usually reached from the town's ferry pier by banca, the traditional Filipino outrigger boat. Big La Laguna Beach, a favourite spot, is situated on the peninsula; its attractive resorts (opposite, above) are backed by a forest of coconut palms (opposite, below). The nearby coral reefs have been well protected for a number of years, and the whole Puerto Galera region is one of the country's best and most popular diving areas. The comings and goings of dive boats are a common sight (middle left) along the local beaches.

Southern Luzon's most famous landmark is the mighty Mount Mayon, with 44 eruptions the most active volcano in the Philippines. Towering over the city of Legaspi (right and top), the volcano sweeps upwards from sea level in an unbroken arc to the summit crater 2421 metres (7941 feet) above, giving rise to its reputation as one of the world's most perfectly symmetrical volcanoes. Despite the constant threat it poses, farmers cannot help but be drawn to the rich soils that surround it, their fields reaching to its very feet (above). The challenging climb to the volcano's summit has also made it a magnet for many visitors.

In the shadow of the massive Mount Mayon sits the city of Legaspi (or Legazpi), named after the Spaniard who in 1565 established the first Spanish settlement in the Philippines. But for its proximity to the country's most active volcano, Legaspi (right) would be a quite ordinary port town. Though daily life, including the traffic of the jeepneys, goes on as normal, there are few places – even in the downtown area – from which the smouldering crater is not visible.

A rice farmer at Malilipot, between Legaspi and Mount Mayon, ploughs his paddy fields prior to planting out seedlings (opposite, above). A steady flow of water is essential to the management of paddy fields, and in most parts of Bicol, as the far south of Luzon is known, water is plentiful. During the dry season, however, water can be in short supply in the towns, necessitating deliveries by tanker (opposite, below left). Near Legaspi, Busay Falls (opposite, below right) consist of seven levels of vertical cascades and pools; the lowest level, shown here, is a popular spot for the locals to bathe.

Almost at Luzon's southern tip in Sorsogon Province lies Bulusan Volcano National Park, an active volcano surrounded by rainforest (above). The park's total area is just less than 3700 hectares (9142 acres), though the forest within it occupies a relatively small proportion of the whole. Much of the forest lies around scenic Bulusan Lake (opposite, above); a footpath around the lake's shores gives plenty of opportunities for exploring. Under the canopy of trees there is some extensive wildlife to be seen, with skinks and butterflies being especially common sights (left and below left).

Off the western coast of Sorsogon Province near the southern tip of Luzon and close to the town of Donsol, a group of about 50 resident Whale Sharks (butanding in Pilipino) has recently been sighted. The town has now set up an ecotourism project to take visitors out to watch and even swim with the sharks (opposite, below). In most parts of the tropics, sightings of Whale Sharks, except from spotter planes, are extremely rare but at Donsol sightings of ten or more in a single morning are just about guaranteed. A wave of excited conservationists and marine biologists has already visited the town to observe these unusual creatures.

THE LAND OF FESTIVALS
THE WESTERN VISAYAS

The group of islands that makes up the western part of the 'waist' of the Philippine archipelago is known as the Western Visayas. Amongst them is the country's most famous destination, the tiny island of Boracay, located off the northern tip of the much larger island of Panay. Boracay attracts more visitors than anywhere else in the country, people coming for the superb beaches and clear waters that are essential components of any tropical island paradise.

The main islands of the group are Panay and Negros; lesser ones include Guimaras and Romblon. Almost all are very rural, growing such crops as sugar cane, rice, mangoes and pineapple. The western part of Panay and the central backbone of Negros are characterized by major mountain ranges – in the case of Negros highly volcanic – which are the last refuges of the area's wildlife.

Boracay has the best developed tourism in the Western Visayas, although in January thousands of people also pour into Kalibo and Iloilo, two of Panay's main towns, for the country's biggest festivals, Ati-Atihan and Dinagyang. Both date back to the 13th century, when ten clans arrived on Panay after fleeing oppression in Borneo. The local Negrito tribe, the Ati, allowed them to take control of large areas of land and thus establish a new home, an event that the people of Panay have celebrated ever since.

To the south of Panay lies Negros, a long rectangular island best known as the sugar cane capital of the country: over half its land is given over to the crop. The largest city in the north of Negros is Bacolod, a convenient starting point for an exploration of Mount Kanlaon, an active volcano surrounded by dense rainforest and the highest mountain in the Visayas. The tough climb to its summit can be rewarded with a soak in the hot springs at Mambucal, a pleasant village set in the cool shade of the forest.

Dumaguete, a relaxed town that is the site of Silliman University, one of the country's most prestigious centres of learning, is situated in the south of Negros. Further down the coast lie a number of beaches, centred mainly around Dauin, as well as Apo Island, famous as the site of some of the country's most spectacular coral reefs, the result of long-term protection under the care of Silliman's Marine Laboratory.

A new marine ecotourism project is located at Bais, not far north of Dumaguete. Situated at the mouth of the Tanon Strait, a narrow but extremely deep stretch of water that separates Negros from Cebu, Bais is the starting point for boat trips to see the local dolphin and whale populations. Sightings of large groups of Spinner Dolphins are almost guaranteed and Pilot Whales and rare Pygmy Sperm Whales are frequently encountered.

PREVIOUS PAGES
Page 92: *A dancer, wearing a traditional costume that recalls those of the aboriginal Negrito people of Panay, performs at Dinagyang, Iloilo's annual festival held at the end of January.*
Page 93: *A paraw, or sailing outrigger, glides gently up to White Beach on Boracay, the island to the north of Panay that is often considered one of the world's most beautiful beach destinations.*

The tiny island of Boracay is the jewel in the crown of Philippine beach destinations. Discovered by travellers some 20 years ago, it now attracts international visitors from around the globe. White Beach (right), the island's longest stretch of sand, is lined with coconut palms and extends along much of the west coast. To date development has been relatively low-key (opposite, below left). Whereas in days gone by there was little to do but sunbathe and swim, now there is much on offer, including the chance to sail a traditional paraw (above). Despite the visitors, some aspects of local life – such as the collecting of sea shells on Yapak Beach in the north of the island (opposite, below right) – continue unchanged.

There can hardly be a more evocative image of the tropics than a beachside coconut palm silhouetted against the sunset (left). At this time of day on Boracay, locals and visitors alike stroll along the beach, enjoying the cool air and watching the changing colours of dusk and approaching night. Even on White Beach, which sometimes appears to be purely the preserve of overseas visitors, the locals continue with their own lives. Each January, in common with every town and village across adjacent Panay, they hold their own Ati-Atihan Festival, parading the beach in costumes and with blackened skins (below left).

Business on White Beach, including setting up small bars right on the edge of the sand (opposite, below left), is run to ensure that visitors rarely need to exert themselves. Inevitably, souvenirs, such as sarongs (opposite, below right) made just about anywhere in South-east Asia, are widely available. Although White Beach is the most popular spot on Boracay, there are other places like attractive Diniwid Beach, just to the north (above), to explore. For those feeling energetic it is possible to tour some of the other beaches by tricycle or boat. Any tour will stop at Yapak Beach, at Boracay's northern tip (opposite, above).

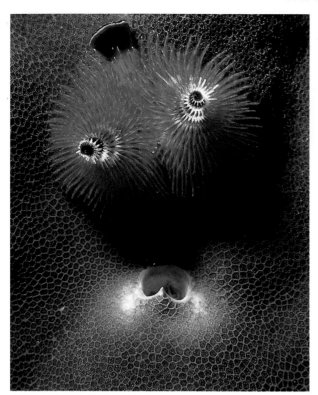

Boracay is best known for its beaches but it also has a very diverse and enjoyable range of dive sites, offering everything from shallow, sheltered coral gardens to deep blue-water sites. At the end of a successful dive (above), divers will have seen abundant varieties of marine life, including numerous different species of fish.

Barrel sponges (opposite, below) are probably the largest marine invertebrates to be encountered, while only a diver with sharp eyes will spot the tiny, colourful Christmas tree worm (opposite, above left). Many fish, such as lionfish (opposite, above right), are exotically patterned or brilliantly coloured. The bright blue of the Ribbon Eel (middle right) identifies it as a male (the females are yellow). Ribbon Eels spend most of their time hiding in crannies in the reef, coming out only occasionally to feed. Fantastically colourful nudibranchs (below right) are molluscs that have no shells; they are usually only about 3–4 centimetres (1⅛–1⅝ inches) long.

Just south of Boracay lies the much larger island of Panay. Throughout the first half of January the town of Kalibo in northern Panay celebrates its annual festival of Ati-Atihan, the finale of which takes place over the third weekend of the month. On these two days the town vibrates to the sound of drums (left) as teams of blackened dancers parade through the crowded streets (below left). Although Ati-Atihan is a pre-Christian festival, religious elements have been absorbed, including the parading of statues of the Santo Niño (Baby Jesus), introduced during the Spanish period (below right).

All the participants at Ati-Atihan dress up in stupendous costumes (opposite) that are created purely for the event; each team competes fiercely to win the coveted prize as the year's best.

Practically every town and village across Panay holds its own Ati-Atihan Festival during January; those held at Kalibo and Iloilo are by far the largest and most renowned. Iloilo's Dinagyang Festival climaxes on the fourth weekend of January with huge processions and dances around the city's streets (left). While Kalibo's event is wild and chaotic, with little crowd control, Iloilo's is well-organized and choreographed.

At Dinagyang, the dance teams, some consisting of over a hundred dancers, move around the town, performing at designated sites. During each performance the teams are judged on both their costumes and their dance routine, the overall winners being announced once the results from the different dance sites have been compared. Competition between teams is extremely fierce, resulting in outlandish costumes and vibrant, complex dance routines (right and far right).

At Iloilo, the dance sites are usually major street intersections at which makeshift viewing stands have been erected (below).

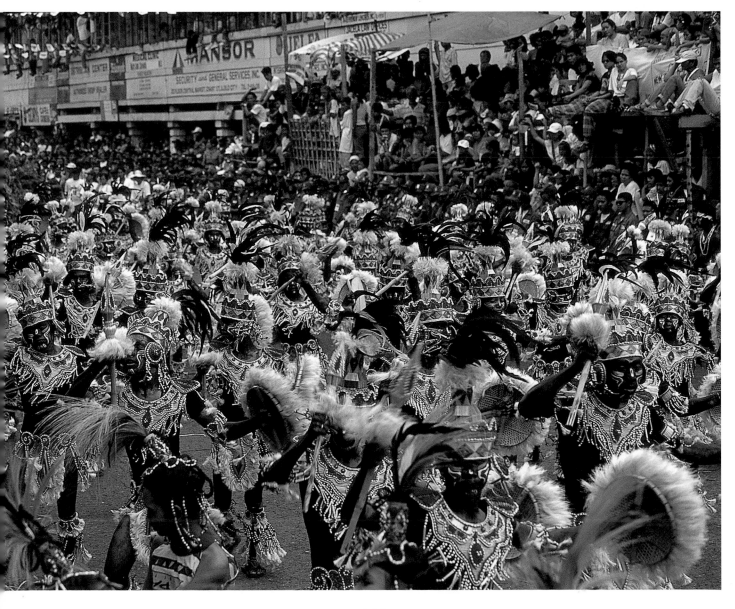

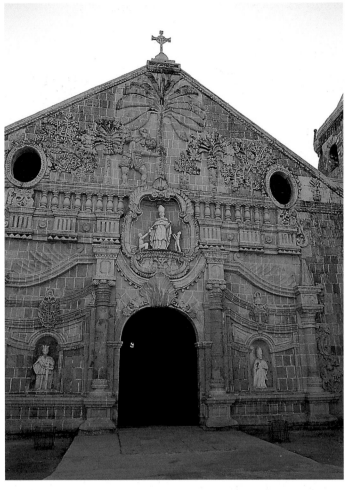

Fishing is the mainstay for many coastal people around the Philippines; the people of Miagao, a small town to the west of Iloilo, are no exception. Much of the fishing relies on the use of outriggers (above), generally small and easily beached, but nets strung out from the beach are also commonly used (left). Miagao is best known for its unique18th-century church, a sturdy and fortress-like structure built to resist both pirates and earthquakes. The uniqueness of the church lies in the superb reliefs that decorate its façade (top). These depict a profusion of tropical vegetation, including coconut palms and papayas, and European-style figures, including Saint Christopher.

On the island of Negros, the city of Bacolod – the capital of Negros Occidental province – was founded on the sugar trade. The Provincial Museum, an attractive building fronted by a park and lake (top), tells the story of the development of the sugar plantations during the 19th century.

One of Bacolod's closest rural attractions is the hot springs resort of Mambucal, which lies in forest on the northern slopes of Mount Kanlaon, an active volcano. Although this is not a protected area, a mass of signs on the edge of the village encourages visitors to look after nature (above). The people of Mambucal, country folk from the hills and farms around, bring baskets of fruit and flowers as their contribution to local festivals (left).

For most of the year Bacolod is very much an affluent working city, but every October it comes alive to Masskara, its annual festival (above). Meaning 'Many Faces', Masskara was conceived in 1980 to dramatize the strength and vitality of the Negrenses (as the people of Negros are called).

The central feature of Masskara is its processions and street dances, in which the participants wear masks depicting happy, smiling faces (right and far right). The festival is a time of both celebration and fierce competition to win the 'best mask' prizes.

Not far south of Bacolod is Mount Kanlaon Natural Park. On the park's western edge, around the village of Guintubdan, there are a number of spectacular waterfalls, including Mag Asawang (above left) and the nearby Oro ('gold') falls. The top of Mag Asawang is fairly easily reached from the village, although the bottom of the falls is virtually unreachable.

Above Guintubdan, once inside the Natural Park, the visitor enters dense rainforest, the lower storey of which is a tangle of rattans, tree ferns, lianas and various shrubs. Flowers are usually few and far between, but one quite common flowering tree is Medinilla magnifica *(left).*

At the heart of Mount Kanlaon Natural Park stands Mount Kanlaon itself. At 2465 metres (8087 feet), it is the highest mountain in the Visayas and an active volcano. Surrounded by dense rainforest, the park is also one of the country's most important protected areas. Over the years the volcanically active area has migrated, leaving the old crater (above) inactive. The currently active crater lies just beyond the ridge.

This proud cockerel (right) has been bred for fighting at a breeding farm in the tiny village of Guintubdan on the lower slopes of Mount Kanlaon. Cockfighting is one of the national sports of the Philippines and many men take great pride in owning a fighting cock. The birds can exchange hands for considerable sums of money, so breeding can be a financially rewarding business. Guintubdan is one of the largest cockerel-breeding centres on Negros, and cockerels far outnumber humans; any visiting hiker will find little opportunity to sleep past four in the morning.

109

On the south coast of Negros lies Dumaguete, a pleasant city which is dominated by Silliman University. It is a relaxed place, with an attractive seafront promenade (left) that is quiet during the day but filled in the evening with students and local residents enjoying the sea breeze. On the downtown streets, the stores are fronted by a plethora of advertising hoardings, many of them used simply to provide some shade (below left). As with many of the smaller Philippine cities, taxis are a rare sight in Dumaguete. Instead, their place is taken by a hoard of motorized tricycles (opposite, below). The city's history goes back several centuries, as this Spanish-era watchtower next to the main market testifies (below). It was built as a lookout point from which to watch for approaching pirates.

One of the liveliest weekly events in the Dumaguete region is the market (opposite, above) held every Wednesday at the seaside village of Malatapay, about 20 kilometres (12 miles) south of the city. Here it is possible to buy everything from a toothbrush to cows and water buffalo.

Off the southern tip of Negros lies tiny Apo Island, a place whose coral reefs have been protected and extensively studied since the 1970s by Silliman University's Marine Laboratory based at Dumaguete. A variety of underwater terrains – from gently sloping areas strewn with large boulders to sheer drop-offs into very deep water – coupled with extremely strong currents has created a great diversity of life. In the deeper waters, shoals of pelagics, such as these Bigeye Trevally (left), are common and often seen swimming in formation.

A dive party prepares to enter the water off Apo Island (below). The Marine Laboratory tries to control the number of divers around Apo, but it is becoming an increasingly popular dive location due to the fine condition of the reef. Some sections can get quite busy with divers (below left), making it all the more important that everyone takes care not to damage the corals. Every day, a number of dive boats from nearby Dumaguete or Dauin can be seen anchored off Apo (opposite, top).

Basking in the sunshine, two Short-finned Pilot Whales lie at the water's surface (above). North of Apo, the Tanon Strait, a narrow but very deep stretch of water separating Negros from Cebu, is home to several species of whales and dolphins. Boat trips from the town of Bais are now a daily occurrence, with sightings of Spinner Dolphins and Pilot Whales very likely.

Apo Island's reefs are home to a startling array of reef fish, many of them, including this brightly coloured Coral Grouper (right), sporting remarkable colours. Such fish are commonly found on many of the reefs of the Philippines but, in places, overfishing has meant that some of those seen are very small. At Apo, however, reef protection and fishing controls have ensured a healthy population of large reef fish, creating a quite magnificent spectacle for divers.

GATEWAY TO THE SOUTH

THE EASTERN VISAYAS

From the wealth and bustle of Cebu City – the country's second commercial centre and unofficial capital of the south – to the remote and little known forests of Samar, the Eastern Visayas is a region of great contrasts. Cebu City is very much the focus for the whole of the Visayan region, with a busy international airport and the Philippines' largest

sea port, as well as extensive air and ferry connections to all the Visayan islands. It is here that many visitors start their tour of the Eastern Visayas.

The main islands of the area are Cebu, Bohol, Leyte, Samar and Masbate. Cebu is a long, narrow island, densely populated and now almost completely deforested. Off it lie a number of smaller islands, of which the best known is Mactan, the site of Cebu City's international airport and luxurious resort hotels. Mactan Island is connected to the Cebu mainland by a bridge, and from here southwards into the centre of Cebu City are industrial zones producing the electronics and textiles that lie at the heart of Cebu's success.

For the visitor, the city's main attractions lie in the old districts close to the port. These include the Basilica Minore del Santo Niño, a church that houses a statue of the Infant Jesus, the oldest Catholic icon in the country, which is said to have been given to the wife of Cebu's chieftain in 1521 by Ferdinand Magellan himself.

Apart from Mactan Island, Cebu's best known resort, and certainly its finest dive area, is Moalboal on the island's southwest coast. There is little beach here but the diving, which is centred mainly around nearby Pescador Island, is excellent.

Beach lovers will want to head east to the island of Bohol, and especially to Alona Beach on Panglao Island at Bohol's southern tip. A serious rival to Boracay, Panglao's beaches are extremely beautiful, while the diving around tiny nearby Balicasag Island is some of the best in the Philippines. Inland, Bohol is famous for the Chocolate Hills, over 1200 small rounded hills so-named due to their colour at the end of the dry season.

To the east of Bohol, Leyte and Samar – twin islands linked by bridge – are less explored. Protecting the Visayas from the forces of the Pacific, they are generally thinly populated. They both retain extensive forests which, it is believed, still support the Philippine Eagle. Close to Tacloban, the largest city on Leyte, Red Beach is famous as the first landing point for American forces arriving to free the Philippines from Japanese occupation towards the end of World War II. Northeast of Tacloban, in the south of Samar, the caves and gorges of Sohoton National Park are being opened up for ecotourism; although occupying a small area, the Park is beautiful and quite unspoilt.

Cebu City was the site of the Philippines' first Spanish settlement. The old part of the city retains many reminders of Spain's 350-year rule, one of the grandest being the Basilica Minore del Santo Niño (opposite, above). A widespread devotion to Catholicism ensures a lively trade for vendors of votive objects (above), especially for stallholders outside the Basilica. Catering for life's daily needs, the colourful Carbon Market, selling a huge array of fresh vegetables (opposite, below), is a focal point of the old city. It is also one of the best places to buy handicrafts and flowers (right).

PREVIOUS PAGES
Page 114: In the rural areas of Bohol, many houses are adorned with flowers, especially bougainvillea and orchids.
Page 115: Fishermen prepare their lines before the next trip out from Pamilacan.

A fine relief (left), depicting the victory of the Christian church over sin, above the entrance to the Basilica Minore del Santo Niño, one of the oldest and most important churches in the Philippines. For sheer colour, however, it is hard to beat the Taoist Temple (top), built in Beverly Hills, one of Cebu's wealthiest suburbs. More than simply a statement of the Chinese community's religious faith, its size is also symbolic of the wealth and success of the local Chinese people.

Cebu gardens – from the Taoist Temple in the suburbs to Fort San Pedro on the sea front – are often endowed with the lovely frangipani tree, whose fragrant flowers (above) are usually a delicate yellowy-white.

Another reminder of Cebu's Spanish past is Fort San Pedro (right), *named after the ship that brought Miguel Legaspi, founder of the Spanish settlement, to Cebu. From this fort Spain controlled the whole Visayan region. Today little remains of the site (much destroyed in World War II), but the setting in an attractive park brings space and greenery to an otherwise crowded part of the city.*

The guitar was a Spanish introduction that clearly struck a chord with the Filipinos. All shapes and sizes of guitar are still widely produced in Cebu, especially on Mactan Island, where it is possible to visit a number of workshops (below).

One of Cebu's most relaxed beach areas is Moalboal, located on the island's south-west coast. Consisting of a string of simple hotels, cottages and restaurants along Panagsama Beach (centre left and above left), *it mostly attracts divers who come to explore the area's superb coral reefs, particularly those around nearby Pescador Island. With many of the buildings standing very close to the shore, hermit crabs are frequently found crawling around among the trees and bungalows* (above). *The beach is several kilometres from the town of Moalboal, so the usual way to get there is by motorized tricycle* (below left).

Mactan Island, close to Cebu City, is Cebu's premier tourist resort. A number of luxury hotels have been built here (opposite, above), *catering largely for overseas visitors on short-stay holidays. Providing every service and comfort imaginable, some also have lush tropical gardens that contain orchids* (opposite, below centre) *and other colourful plants. Mactan souvenirs include a great array of shell crafts, such as hanging decorations and lampshades* (opposite, below left). *Near the northern tip of the island stands a monument to Ferdinand Magellan* (opposite, below right), *who first claimed the Philippines for Spain. He was killed close to this spot in April 1521 by Lapu-Lapu, the local chieftain. Another monument, dedicated to Lapu-Lapu, stands nearby.*

The island of Bohol, which lies south-east of Cebu, is renowned for its old Spanish churches. The oldest of them all, dating from 1727, is the Church of the Immaculate Conception (top) at Baclayon, a town on Bohol's south coast just east of the island's capital, Tagbilaran. In the countryside the churches are often among the few buildings made of stone. Ordinary village houses (above) are usually constructed from a coconut-timber frame, walls of woven coconut leaf matting, and a thatched roof made from nipa palm leaves.

Despite its idyllic outlook, necessity probably led to the construction of this house in the mangroves (right). For badly off families, building out over unclaimed waters avoids the struggle to find funds to buy or rent land.

Inland Bohol is overwhelmingly rural, with small villages and their modest farms surrounded by quite extensive secondary forests. For the farmers of the island, rice cultivation is an important activity. Preparing the fields and then planting out the rice seedlings (left) is a labour-intensive task. Water buffalo, widely used to plough the rice fields, spend their time when not at work tethered in pastures, almost invariably accompanied by the aptly named Cattle Egret (centre left).

The church at Corella (top left), a small village north of Tagbilaran, is typical of many in Bohol: a fine Spanish colonial structure and by far the largest and grandest building in the village.

The Chocolate Hills (above) are one of the Philippines' best known landscape features, and are quite unique to the country. Situated close to the centre of Bohol near the town of Carmen, their name comes from the colour they take on towards the end of the dry season when much of their covering of grass has died. Their geological origin is uncertain, though it is believed that they were formed by the weathering of limestone lying over impermeable clays. Local mythology has two much more colourful legends, one claiming that the hills represent the tears of a giant who was thwarted in love, the other saying that this was the battlefield of two giants, more than 1200 hills being the damage they left behind.

The wooded areas of Bohol contain an interesting variety of wildlife, including the Pompadour Green Pigeon (right).

Panglao Island, off the south-western corner of Bohol, has several fine beaches, including the white-sand Alona Beach (opposite). Despite being a potential rival to Boracay, expansion of tourism on Panglao has been deliberately slow and very low-key to prevent overcrowding. Some development has taken place along Alona Beach, but the cottages and restaurants remain rustic and in harmony with their surroundings (above).

Volleyball is a popular sport among Filipinos, and it is common, on Alona Beach and elsewhere, to see workers and visitors alike enjoying a game on the beach during the cool of the late afternoon (right).

127

One of the main attractions of Alona Beach is the diving, which is among the best in the Philippines. The main dive area is around nearby Balicasag Island, a tiny 12-hectare (29-acre) coralline islet a few kilometres to the south-west. Designated a Marine Park, it has beautiful protected reefs and deep waters around them teeming with life. Ringed with a spectacular white beach (opposite, top), Balicasag is also a perfect place for beach lovers; its clear, shallow waters close to the shore make an ideal spot for novice diver practice (left).

Balicasag Island's underwater world consists principally of a short, gently sloping reef followed by an abrupt wall that drops vertically into extremely deep water. There is a great diversity of healthy corals and reef fish, including grouper, triggerfish and soldierfish; shoals of pelagics, including jack, barracuda and tuna, are plentiful. Gorgonian sea fans, fan-shaped corals that vary from a few centimetres to a couple of metres across, are widespread. When viewed close up, their branching surfaces reveal a mass of tiny polyps covered with stinging tentacles (left). One type of Gorgonian sea fan is the red Acabaria species (opposite, middle right). Living among the corals are many other invertebrates, including the blue sea squirts, Ropalaea crassa (opposite, middle left).

The reef around Pamilacan Island, the 'nesting place of Manta Rays', also boasts a good variety of marine life. Reached in an hour by boat from Alona Beach, it is home to a community dependent on the sea's bounty (right). This community is one of the few in the Philippines that still hunts whales, Whale Sharks and Manta Rays, all of which are found around the island. In an effort to persuade the people to swap their harpoons for visitors with cameras and binoculars, the Philippine branch of the World Wide Fund for Nature is currently running a programme to promote whale-watching ecotourism here.

East of Bohol lies the much larger island of Leyte. Tacloban, its capital, is home to 140,000 people and is the largest city on the island. The hill that overlooks the city is topped by a statue of Christ, and on the way up to the summit there are representations of the Twelve Stations of the Cross (left).

Sitting on an east-facing bay and sheltered by the island of Samar visible in the distance, Tacloban (below) is small by comparison to other provincial capitals and something of a quiet backwater.

Just south of Tacloban at Palo, a floodlit statue depicts General Douglas MacArthur and his distinguished men wading ashore in October 1944 to liberate the Philippines from Japanese control (right). The statue captures a moment forever famous among Filipinos, the fulfillment of MacArthur's promise when he fled the invading Japanese in 1942: 'I shall return.' The statue stands in MacArthur Park, alongside Red Beach, the site of the first massive American landings that the General planned and led.

Across the strait from Tacloban on the island of Samar is the small town of Basey, from where boats can be hired (below) to travel upriver to Sohoton National Park.

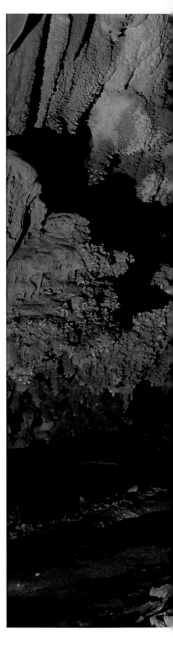

Fishing boats travel along the beautiful palm-lined river that leads into the interior of Samar towards Sohoton National Park (top left). The river offers the best route into the National Park; boats can be hired either in Basey at the river's mouth or in Tacloban on the opposite side of the strait separating Samar from Leyte. Once inside the park, the landscape is one of limestone gorges with weirdly shaped rocks and dense vegetation that hangs right down to the water (above left).

The National Park covers only 800 hectares (1977 acres) but it is home to a variety of wildlife, including Long-tailed Macaques (left). In the Philippines these are sometimes called Philippine Macaques; they are the same species as the Long-tailed Macaques found throughout South-east Asia, but it is thought that they may be a separate subspecies.

The main attraction in Sohoton National Park is its caves, known locally as 'wonder caves', which have been inhabited sporadically since prehistoric times. One of the largest and most impressive is Panhulugan Cave, which is filled with stalactites and stalagmites (above), all still in a pristine natural state. There is no electric light or other visitor facilities in the caves, but park rangers with oil lamps act as guides. The park can be further explored by boat and foot, but the river must be quite high for this; when water levels are low, it is not possible to penetrate much further upriver. Here, a guide and boat crew stand in the shallows, their boat grounded by low water (right).

THE ISLANDS OF THE SOUTH
MINDANAO AND THE SULU ARCHIPELAGO

Mindanao and the Sulu Islands were long considered the 'Wild West' of the Philippines. Always the first areas to flare up in difficult times, for years travelling here was considered unsafe. For most of Mindanao, all that has changed, the treaties signed in the early 1990s between the government and two principal rebel groups bringing peace and an economic boom. Travel has since become much safer, although visitors are advised to exercise caution when visiting the west and the Sulu Islands.

The island of Mindanao consists of two mainland masses joined by a narrow isthmus. One area of Mindanao particularly loved by Filipinos is Camiguin, a jewel of an island off Mindanao's north coast. Blessed with a beautiful coastline and stunning mountain scenery, its people are very friendly and the entire place exudes a feeling of well-being.

Off north-eastern Mindanao lies Siargao Island, now a protected area due to its remaining rainforests, massive mangrove area and wonderful coastline. Although most visitors come to Siargao for the surf, the island has many other attractions, especially its beaches, the best of which lie on a scattering of offshore desert islets.

Far to the south-east of Mindanao is Davao, the second largest city in the country and the third most important economically. Davao serves as the gateway to a number of nearby places of interest, including Samal Island, where there is a series of pleasant beaches and resorts. North of the city, at Malagos, is the Philippine Eagle Nature Center, where efforts are being made to breed the endangered Philippine Eagle in captivity. The forested mountains of Mindanao, including Mount Apo, to the west of Davao, and the Mount Kitanglad range in the island's centre, are the main haunt of this rare bird. At 2956 metres (11,256 feet), Apo is the highest mountain in the Philippines. An inactive volcano and a national park, it is surrounded by one of the country's most important rainforests.

Lying at the westernmost tip of Mindanao, the city of Zamboanga is a Christian enclave at the heart of the Islamic part of the island. Zamboanga is famous for its *vintas*, outrigger boats with brightly coloured sails; the city is also the starting point for trips to the Sulu Islands.

Some parts of the Sulu archipelago are less easy to reach but one of the most accessible and attractive areas for visitors is in and around Bongao, the main town of Tawi-Tawi. From here it is a simple boat ride to Sitangkai, a town built entirely on stilts over a coral reef and one of the closest Philippine settlements to Borneo. The people in this entire region are Moslem, another facet of the diversity of the southern islands.

Just to the north of Mindanao lies the small island of Camiguin. Its northern coastline is an almost continuous stretch of volcanic sand (above) which, around the village of Agoho, is overlooked by Mount Hibok-Hibok, the only active volcano among the island's seven. Shortly before sunset, people come out onto the beach to enjoy the evening air (opposite, above and below) and to prepare their fishing tackle. In the morning, many hands gather to make light work of bringing in the catch; one of the most frequently caught fish is tuna (left).

PREVIOUS PAGES
Page 134: At festival time in Zamboanga, the local outriggers known as vintas sport strikingly patterned and brilliantly coloured sails.
Page 135: Orchids and bougainvillaea fill the gardens on Camiguin Island.

Many of Camiguin's attractions are found along the coast but there are beautiful places inland too, including waterfalls and hot and cold springs. Katibawasan Falls (left), a spectacular ribbon of water that cascades 50 metres (164 feet) into a pool below, lies in a small area of forest at the foot of Mount Hibok-Hibok. On the edge of a plantation near the mountain, hot springs feed this small lake (bottom).

The people of Camiguin have a love of flowers and take pride in their gardens. In most villages on the island the gardens of even the simplest homes are filled with a profusion of orchids and other tropical flowers (below).

As in most rural areas of the Philippines, the architecture of the island is simple and often elegant, as exemplified by this house (right) *near Mambajao, the island's capital. The house is raised off the ground to protect it from vermin, the walls are built of coconut timber and the roof is thatched with nipa palm. The hedge of croton plants that encloses the garden is a feature frequently seen on Camiguin.*

Camiguin is somewhat off the beaten track, so a visitor photographing an orchid garden is certain to generate a fascinated and friendly audience (below). *The market in Mambajao, near the tiny dock, is full of agricultural produce and food stalls, overseen by colourful and equally good-natured characters* (bottom).

139

The whole of Siargao Island, off the north-eastern tip of Mindanao, is now a national park. It has been so designated to protect both its important habitats, which range from lowland rainforest to a huge mangrove swamp, and its beautiful coastline. For most of Siargao's inhabitants life revolves around subsistence fishing, with even the youngest members of the family frequently giving a hand (above left).

Siargao can be reached by boat from Surigao, the provincial capital on the Mindanao mainland. Like almost every town in the country, Surigao has a cockfighting stadium (left). Fights are social events for the local men, with part of the enjoyment provided by the long build-up to each fight, during which members of the audience signal bets to each other with different hand and finger gestures.

During a religious festival held at the town of General Luna on Siargao Island, people from outlying islands bring holy images (above) from their own churches to be blessed at the local cathedral.

The beautiful white beaches of Siargao (right) are matched by those on the tiny nearby islands of Dako, Guyam and Mamon, all of which can be reached by outrigger from Siargao.

On its way to the open sea, a freighter sails through the narrow strait that separates Davao from Samal Island (above), the site of the city's beaches and new beach resorts. Although Davao, on the south-eastern coast of Mindanao, is the country's second largest city, years of local unrest in the region held back its economy. Since the coming of peace in the early 1990s, commercial development and visitor numbers have increased dramatically.

A news stand in downtown Davao shows a range of newspapers and magazines, almost all of which are in English (left).

Davao's Buddhist Longhua Temple (top right) *is indicative of the presence of a successful Chinese community in the city. Often running shops and import-export businesses, the Filipino Chinese are prominent in urban economies throughout the country. Close to the temple are the Puentaspina Orchid Gardens* (middle right). *Davao is known for its orchids and this is one of the best places to see a fine display.*

Outside Davao Cathedral, young brides-maids await the bride (right). *Weddings are often glamorous events, with the women and girls in beautiful, flamboyant dresses and the men wearing the traditional Filipino shirt, the* Barong Tagalog.

Close to Davao, Mount Apo, an inactive volcano and the highest mountain in the Philippines, is at the centre of a 70,000-hectare (172,970-acre) national park, one of the country's largest and most important. From the summit of the mountain, the extent of the rainforest that covers its sides can be clearly seen (opposite, top). The Marbel River (left), which tumbles down its middle slopes, cuts a swathe through the dense rainforest. Anyone who climbs Mount Apo from the west becomes intimately familiar with this river as, for part of the route, its course is the only way up, the fast-moving waters needing to be forded no less than 12 times. The hike to the summit (opposite, middle left) is becoming one of the most popular trails in the Philippines, even though it is a steep two to three-day climb up and down. But once the hike is over, a soak in the hot spring at Lake Agco (opposite, bottom left), which marks the end of the trail, will soothe away aches and pains.

Mount Apo Natural Park is the home of small numbers of Philippine Eagles (opposite, below right) in the wild, as well as other endangered species. The nearby Philippine Eagle Nature Center is attempting to breed these magnificent birds in captivity, in order to release them back into the wild.

The areas around Davao are home to a number of cultural minorities, including the Mandayas, Mansakas, Bagobos, Kalagans and Manobos. One of the largest of these groups, the Mandaya people (right) are renowned for their craft traditions of weaving, pottery and silver work. Worn mostly at festival times, the colourful clothing of the farming and hunter-gathering Bagobos (below) is traditionally ornamented with beads and shells.

To the west of the Mount Apo range lies a vast plain, spreading across parts of North Cotabato, Magunidanao and Lanao del Sur provinces. Part of this region is occupied by the Liguasan Marsh, the country's largest freshwater swamp and an important refuge for wildlife. Large areas of drier land are given over to rice cultivation. When the time comes for the labour-intensive job of threshing each crop of rice, every generation lends a hand (opposite, above) and the rice is taken away on buffalo-drawn sledges (opposite, below).

To the north of the Liguasan Marsh stands the Mount Kitanglad range, the site of Mount Dulang-Dulang, at 2938 metres (9639 feet) the Philippines' second highest peak. Like Mount Apo, the Mount Kitanglad Range Natural Park is part of the World Bank-funded Conservation of Priority Protected Areas Project (CPPAP) and is a known site for Philippine Eagles. The trail up Mount Kitanglad's slopes passes for some considerable distance through scrubby grasslands (top right), the home to innumerable small mammals, insects and spiders (above). At the edge of the forest, however, there are excellent views of the trees and the great shanks of Old Man's Beard draped over many of them (top left).

Once in the forest, it is difficult to get an uninterrupted view of anything. The only solution is to look upwards for a sight of the tall tree trunks (left), many of which are used as supports by a variety of climbing plants including huge pandanus.

The upper slopes of the mountains in the Mount Kitanglad range still have a green forest covering, but the middle and lower slopes are a mixture of grasslands, farms and the occasional cluster of trees (above). The forests of even this remote range are now being put under pressure from the increasing human population, which has grown dramatically in recent years due to resettlement in the area of victims of the Mount Pinatubo eruption.

Farmers have brought their animals with them to the area, so buffaloes, perhaps cooling off in a muddy pool (right), are a frequent sight along the trails of the mountain range.

On the quay in the city of Cagayan de Oro, on the north coast of Mindanao, workers move huge sacks filled with the crushed outer shells of coconuts (above), which are used as cooking fuel or fertiliser. The work of loading and off-loading the boats is carried out manually, as is the case in most Philippine ports.

Across the Bohol Sea from Cagayan de Oro, the restful bay at Dapitan (left) lies on Mindanao's north-west coast. Historically, Dapitan is famed as the place of exile to which national hero José Rizal was sent by the Spanish in 1892; he remained here until he was recalled to Manila in 1896 for trial and execution.

Aliguay Island is a tiny speck of land lying off Dapitan. Few visitors come to the island, so life remains much as it has always been. The children (below) *are inquisitive, keen to watch anything unusual happening, but can become suddenly shy at the sight of a stranger. The men keep a few well fed and groomed fighting cocks* (right) *for Sunday sport.*

Aliguay is blessed with excellent beaches and coral reefs. The people live by fishing and farming, and during the day the fishermen relax in the shade by their boats and nets (bottom), *waiting for the evening fishing to begin in the well-stocked seas.*

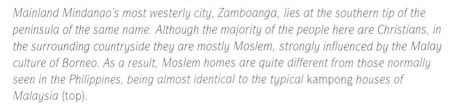

Mainland Mindanao's most westerly city, Zamboanga, lies at the southern tip of the peninsula of the same name. Although the majority of the people here are Christians, in the surrounding countryside they are mostly Moslem, strongly influenced by the Malay culture of Borneo. As a result, Moslem homes are quite different from those normally seen in the Philippines, being almost identical to the typical kampong houses of Malaysia (top).

In the Zamboanga market, even selling a few mangoes can be a sociable event requiring the gathering of a group of friends (above), a scene re-enacted in almost every market across the country. A sight unique to Zamboanga is the vintas, sailing outriggers often adorned with dazzling multi-coloured sails (right). When the vintas are at work, fishing in inshore or coastal waters, standard, plain sails are sported, but at festival time, or when giving rides to visitors, the dramatic patterned sails are hoisted.

To the south of Zamboanga and on the edge of the Sulu archipelago, the large island of Basilan is inhabited mainly by the Islamic Yakan cultural minority. The inland economy consists mostly of rubber, coffee and dates, while the waters around the island are rich fishing grounds, reached from the harbour at Isabela, the island's capital (above left). In the market, shellfish and farmed seaweed are sold by fishing families (left).

The town of Sitangkai is built entirely on stilts in shallow water over a coral reef (above). One of the remotest Philippine communities, it sits beyond the southernmost tip of Tumindao Island, the furthest flung corner of the Sulu archipelago and only 60 kilometres (37 miles) from Borneo. Not surprisingly, this wholly Islamic Malay community has far more dealings with the Malaysian state of Sabah than with almost any part of the Philippines.

Seaweed, used not only for cooking but also as a base for a vast range of industrial products, is farmed extensively in the shallow waters over the Sulu archipelago's coral reefs. An important component of the regional economy, it is carried in large baskets (right) straight from the sea to Basilan's Isabela market.

AN UNSPOILT OUTPOST

PALAWAN

Palawan, a long narrow island on the far south-western fringes of the Philippines, has frequently been dubbed the country's 'final frontier'. The numerous small offshore islands that surround it make up the rest of Palawan province. Large areas of the region are still forested, roads are few and far between and there is only one city, Puerto Princesa,

the rapidly growing provincial capital, on Palawan Island.

For visitors, the appeal of Palawan lies in its unspoilt natural beauty: its forests, bays, beaches, cliffs and coral reefs, many of which are now protected. The nearest natural attraction to Puerto Princesa on the main island is St Paul's Underground River which passes through a spectacular limestone cave. It is accessed from Sabang, a simple village with a magnificent beach.

Further north is El Nido, an area becoming internationally renowned for its stunningly beautiful, island-studded Bacuit Bay. The limestone Bacuit archipelago ranges from small jagged outcrops to islands surrounded by huge, sheer cliffs and deserted beaches. Boats are easily hired to tour the bay: one of the highlights is the lagoon on Miniloc Island, where turtles can frequently be seen.

Off the north-eastern coast of mainland Palawan lie the Calamian Islands, the largest of which is Busuanga. Coron, the main town in the area, is situated on Busuanga, and from

here visits can be made to other islands in the group, including Coron Island and Calauit Island. For divers, the town is also the starting point for trips to the wrecks that fill Coron Bay. This is one of the best wreck-diving sites in east Asia, created by an American bombing raid which sank a fleet of Japanese supply ships here in 1944.

Coron Island, a jagged limestone island similar to those found at El Nido, is inhabited by the Tagbanua people, a shy cultural minority. Only one part of the island is open to visitors, the beautiful Cayangan Lake.

Calauit Island, to the north of Busuanga, is a unique wildlife sanctuary, in that it is home to several species of African mammals, brought here in the 1970s when there were fears for their survival in their native Kenya. The animals roam freely around the island, together with native wildlife. The rangers organise daily tours, which guarantee good sightings of zebra, giraffe and eland.

For marine life, one of the most important sites is the Tubbataha Reef, a vast area of coral shoals in the Sulu Sea nine hours by ship from Puerto Princesa. A national marine park that has been only lightly damaged by dynamite fishing, it is home to a vast array of marine creatures, from the tiniest corals to huge sharks and rays. Far out to sea, it is generally visited only by live-aboard dive boats, which come to the area between March and May.

The little village of Sabang, on Palawan's north-western coast, is the starting point for a trip to St Paul's Underground River National Park. Along the shoreline between Sabang and the park boundary stand strange rock formations (top left)*; at the park,* local *bancas* (above left) *take visitors through the extraordinary limestone caves and chambers through which the underground river runs. It is claimed to be the world's longest such river.*

PREVIOUS PAGES
Page 156: *The luxurious Lagen Island Resort, built on a densely forested island in the Bacuit archipelago, aims to be an environmentally friendly development.*
Page 157: *Far out in the Sulu Sea near Arena Reef, children on a seaweed farm lead unavoidably isolated lives.*

Inland from Sabang's glorious stretch of sand (above), trails lead to the forested hills of the national park. Sabang is reached by jeepney along small roads and, with just a few cottages providing accommodation and amenities for visitors, it remains the sleepy, unspoilt village that it has always been.

Local life around Sabang follows an uncomplicated pattern. Boats are maintained and painted (right) and young boys swim and make toys from jetsam (opposite, bottom).

159

The town of Taytay, situated in the north of Palawan and once the provincial capital, is guarded by the ruins of an old Spanish fort (top). Its walls were made from local coral, as can be clearly seen from the patterns in some of its stones (above). The town sits on a calm, peaceful bay, its 'suburbs' consisting of a fishing village built on piles along the shoreline (opposite, below). At low tide it is a long walk across mud flats to any boats that might be heading out to the islands that stud the bay (opposite, above).

Malampaya Sound near Taytay is one of the major fishing centres of the Philippines; whole families work together to put out the nets (right) and bring in the catch.

Bacuit Bay, generally known as El Nido after the name of the local town, is situated in the far north of Palawan. A sheltered stretch of water studded with limestone islands blessed with forests, beaches and sheer cliffs, the area is rapidly becoming famous – despite its isolation – for its great beauty. Tourism has arrived only in the last few years, but already there are a number of simple guesthouses and, for visitors looking for comfort, several luxurious resorts on the islands in the bay. The town of El Nido itself is a small, quiet place, stretching along an attractive beach on the mainland and backed by stunning cliffs (top). For El Nido's children, plenty of time is spent splashing around in the shallow, clear waters (above). At dusk, the scene is equally idyllic as the sun sets behind Cadlao Island in the bay (left).

Miniloc Island Resort (right), in a perfect setting on Miniloc Island, was one of the first luxury resorts to open in the El Nido area. Others have been springing up around the bay, providing work for many (above) but also posing a concern for the very beauty visitors come to enjoy. However, El Nido has been designated a protected area, and hopes are high that future development will be planned to minimise environmental impact. Miniloc is one of the bay's most beautiful islands; its lagoon (top), ringed by jagged cliffs, is accessible only from the sea and boats have to squeeze through a narrow gap between cliffs to reach it.

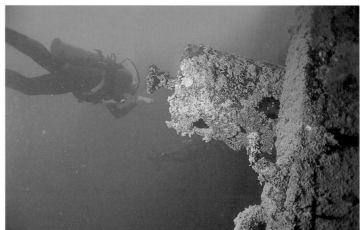

The fine view across Coron town on the island of Basuanga encompasses Coron Bay and, in the distance, Coron Island (opposite, above). *The main centre in the Calamian Islands, the northernmost part of Palawan, Coron town is the access point for visits to Coron Bay and the wildlife sanctuary on Calauit Island, as well as for dive trips to the Coron Bay wrecks and other dive sites. One of the most astonishing underwater sights in the area is Gunter's Cathedral, a submerged cavern off the southern tip of Coron Island* (right).

For divers of all abilities, Coron Bay is something of a paradise, for it is littered with wrecks, most of them the remains of Japanese ships sunk by American bombers towards the end of World War II. Lying among a group of small islands a two-hour boat ride west of Coron town, the wrecks are mainly Japanese supply freighters, although there is also a warship, the Akitsushima. Visibility is not great, but the wrecks are quite spectacular. All are encrusted with marine life, including hard corals and stinging hydroids, and there are many reef fish to be seen, such as lionfish and stonefish (opposite, middle and bottom right). Other wrecks in the area include an old fishing boat (opposite, below left), *which lies in shallow water off the northwest shore of Coron Island.*

Coron town, situated on Busuanga, the largest of the Calamian Islands, is a small, friendly place. Most of it is built on dry land, spreading along the shoreline of Coron Bay, but parts are built on piles out over the water (above and opposite), *including most of the guesthouses. A settlement of Badjao people is found in a separate part of the town; this area too is built out over the water, since the animist beliefs of the Badjao, often known as 'sea gypsies', dictate that they cannot live on land. Their dead are buried on 'graveyard islands' and burials are the only occasions on which the Badjao go ashore.*

Coron Island, across the bay from Coron town, is largely uninhabited. There are several hidden fresh-water lakes on the island, but Cayangan Lake (left) is the only accessible one. It is a beautiful spot with turquoise water surrounded by high limestone pinnacles. The lake is fed by a hot spring, so for divers it is a unique site with the temperature increasing as one dives deeper, reaching 40 °C (104 °F) at 30 metres (98 feet). Although it is a freshwater lake, some marine species are found on its seaward side, including a lone barracuda which is sufficiently used to human beings to be hand-fed. The lake is also known as Barracuda Lake on account of this fish.

In 1976 Calauit, the northernmost island in the Calamian group, was designated a wildlife sanctuary (above). Eight species of African wildlife, believed to be in danger of extinction in Kenya, were introduced here to a habitat similar to their original African one but free of poachers and predators. The African wildlife thrived on Calauit Island, and today herds of giraffe and zebra wander freely over much of it (left and above left). Other African species that were introduced here include impala, waterbuck, bushbuck and eland.

The native wildlife on Calauit has also benefitted from the island's protected status, especially the Calamian Deer (far right), *an animal unique to the Calamian islands that was on the verge of extinction in the 1970s. Today, over a thousand deer live on Calauit and they have also been reintroduced to other islands in the group. Local rangers have captively bred other seriously endangered species, including the Palawan Peacock Pheasant (near right).*

171

Due to their remote location in the middle of the Sulu Sea, the two reefs that make up Tubbataha Reef, a marine national park, are home to some of the Philippines' most diverse underwater life. Divers can witness a huge array of corals and reef fish and, in the surrounding deep waters, almost every type of pelagic, from sharks, manta rays, tuna and barracuda to turtles, dolphins and whales. A typical undersea reef scene reveals brightly coloured soft tree corals, like this Dendronephthya species (above).

The nearest human settlement to Tubbataha Reef is an isolated seaweed farm (right) at Arena Reef, 80 kilometres (50 miles) to the north. With no actual land to build on, the farm's houses are constructed on piles in the shallow water; the seaweed-growing plots are spread over a great area and all maintenance and harvesting must be done by outrigger boat.

INDEX

Page numbers in **bold** type refer to illustrations.

Abu Bakr, Sayyid 25
Abu Sayyaf separatist group 28, 41
Acabaria sp. **128**
Aeta *see* Negrito people
Agco Lake, Mindanao Island **144**
Agoho, Camiguin Island **136**
Aglipayan Independent Church *see* Philippine Independent Church
Agno River **31**
agriculture 17, 18-19, 21, 24, **24**, 30-31, **30**, 32, 36, 37, **37**, 38, 43, **56**, 57, 62, **64-6**, 69, 80, **86**, 88, 93, **124**, **146**, **149** 154
Aguinaldo, Emilio 27
Agusan Marsh Wildlife Sanctuary 17, **20**, 40
Agusan River 13, 40
Aliguay Island **151**
Alona Beach, Bohol Island 115, **126-8**
alphabets 26, 33
Ambuklao Lake **60**
America 28, 35
American colonial period 11, 17, 18, 19, 21, 22, 27, 32, 33, 38, 43
amphibian species 14
Angeles, North Luzon **54**
Anilao, South Luzon 69, **82-3**
animism 22, 23, **62**
Apayao people 21
Apo, Mount 12, 40, 135, **144** Mount Apo Natural Park 17, **144-5**
Apo Island 93, **112-13**
Apo Reef Marine Wildlife Sanctuary 18, **18**
Aquino, Benigno and Corazon 28
Aquino, Francisca Reyes 32
Arab people 25, 41
archaeological finds 24, 41
architecture **26**, 36, **42**, **47**, **71**, **105**, **110**, **122**, **124**, **139**
Arena Reef, Sulu Sea **157**, **172-3**
art and sculpture 27, **33**, 34, **70**, **118**, **130-31**
Asian Short-clawed Otter 15
Ati people 93
Ati-Atihan Festival **7**, 24, 93, **96**, **100-103**
Austronesian people 21, 22, 24

Babuyan Islands 36
Baclayon, Bohol Island 17, **122**
Bacolod, Negros Island 93, **106-7**
Bacuit archipelago 41, **156**, 157
Bacuit Bay, Palawan Island *see* El Nido Bay
Badjao people 21, 23, **168**
Bagobo people **10**, 21, **147**
Baguio, North Luzon 24, 31, 37, 57, **58**, **60**
Bais, Negros Island 93, **113**
Balangao people **62**
Balayan Bay, South Luzon **82**
Balicasag Island 40, 115, **128**
the *balikbayan* 31

Banahaw, Mount 38
Banaue, North Luzon 21, **24**, 37, **56**, 57, **64-7**
banca boats **44**, **82**, **84**, **158-9**
barangay village groups 24, 29
barong pilipino shirts **143**
barracuda 16, **128**, **168**, **172**
Barracuda Lake *see* Coron Lake
barrel sponges **99**
Basco, Batan Island **42**
Basey, Samar Island **131**
Basilan island group 12, 41, **154-5**
Basilica Minore del Santo Niño, Cebu Island 22, **22**, 23, 115, **116**, **118**
basketry 34, **57**, **58**, **155**
bat species 14, 18, 43, **52**
Bataan peninsula 27
Batad, North Luzon **64**
Batanese Islands 12, **20**, 21, 36, **36**, **42**, 43, **44-5**
Batangas, South Luzon 38, 39, **82**, **84**
batfish 16
Bauang, North Luzon **48**
beaches and coastal areas **6**, 7, 13, **14**, 27, **27**, **38**, 39-40, **39**, 41, 43, **48**, **51**, 69, **84**, **93**, **93**, **95-6**, 115, **120**, **127-9**, 135, **136**, **141**, **142**, **151**, 157, **159**, **163**
Benguet pine 37, **37**
Bicol dialect 22
Bicol region, Luzon 38-9
Bigeye Trevally **112**
Binturong (Bearcat) 15, **15**
bird species 14-15, **15**, 17, 18, 43, **52**, 135
Black Nazarene Festival 23, **73**
Blacktip Reef Shark 16
bleeding heart pigeons 14, **52**
Blue Wrasse 16
Blue-naped Parrot 14
boats and ships 26, **38**, **39**, **44**, **48**, **50**, 76, **82**, **84**, **93**, **95**, **105**, **113**, **131-3**, **134**, 135, **136-7**, **141**, **142**, **150-54**, 157, **158-9**, **160-61**, **163**
Bohol Island 12, 14, **17**, 26, 40, **114**, 115, **122-5**
Bohol Sea **150**
Bongao, Tawi-Tawi island 135
Bonifacio, Andres 26, 27
Bontoc, North Luzon 57, **63**
Bontoc people 21, 57, **62**
Boracay Island **6**, 7, **14**, 39-40, **39**, 93, **93**, **95-9**
Borneo 12, 15, 17, 18, 21, 23, 25, 41, **80**, 93, 135, **152**, **155**
bougainvillaea **135**
brasswork 34
Brunei empire 25
Buddhism 22, 23, **143**
buffalo 14, **124**, **146**, **149**
bulol carvings 34
Bulusan, Mount and Lake 39, 69, **90**
burial customs 57, **63**, 68
burnay pots **47**
Busay Falls, South Luzon **88**
Bushbuck **170**
Busuanga Island 157
Butuan, Mindanao Island 24

Cadlao Island **2**
Cagayan de Oro, Mindanao Island **150**
Cagayan River 13, 24, 37
Calabarzon region, South Luzon 38
Calamian Islands **20**, 21, 41, 157
Calamian Deer 14, **171**
Calauit Island 41, 157, **167**, **170-71**
Calabarzon region, South Luzon 38, 69
calesa carriages **3**, **26**, **47**
Camiguin Island 24, 40, 135, **136-9**
cañao rites 67
Carbon Market, Cebu City **116**
Catanduanes Island 39
Cattle Egret **124**
caves **133**, 157, **158**, **167**
Cayangan Lake, Coron Island 157
Cebu City 22, **22**, 23, 24, 25, **25**, 40, **40**, 115, **116-18**
Cebu Island 12, 13, 17, 25, 31, 40, 93, 115, **116-20**
Cebuano dialect 22
children 17, 19, **19**, 20, **20**, **22**, 32, 58, 60, 70, 88, 94, **129**, 137, 139, **140**, **143**, **146-7**, **151**, **157**, **158**, **163**
Children's Island **51**
China 11, 18, 23, 24
Chinese dialects 22
Chinese people **19**, 20, 24, 25, 26, 34, 35, **40**, 41, **118**, 143
Chocolate Hills, Bohol Island 40, 115, **125**
Christianity 11, 18-19, 22-3, 25-6, **62**, **105**, 115, **116**, **118**, **122**, **124**, **130**, 135, **141**, **152**
Christmas tree worm **99**
Church of the Immaculate Conception, Bohol Island **122**
churches and temples 22, **40**, **42**, 55, **105**, 115, **116**, **118**, **122**, **124**, **143**
Clark Field, Manila 31, 38, 43
climatic conditions 13-14, 17, 21, 37, 41, **44**, **54**, 57
Club John Hay, North Luzon 57, **58**
cock fighting **109**, **140**, **151**
coconut palms 30, **30**, 35-6, **84**, **95**, **96**, **132**, **150**
coffee 36, **154**
cold springs **138**
communism 28, 40
conservation projects 17-18, **17**
copper mining 31
Coral Grouper **113**
coral reefs 13, **13**, **14**, 16, **16**, 17, 18, 36, 38, 39, 40, 41, **48**, 69, **82-3**, **85**, 93, **99**, **112-13**, **120**, **128-9**, 135, **151**, **155**, 157, **157**, **161**, **167**, **172**
Cordillera Central Mountains 12, **21**, 31, 34, 36, 37, **37**, 57, **60-67**
Coron, Busuanga Island 157, **166-9**
Coron Island 157, **166**, **168**
Coron Lake **168**
Corregidor Island 27
costume **64**, **67**, **92**, **96**, **100-103**, **107**, **143**, **147**

crabs **120**
crafts 34, **47**, **57**, **58**, **117**, **120**, **147**
Crested Serpent-Eagle **77**
crocodile species 14, 40
croton plants **139**
cultural identity 21, 23, 26, 32, 33, 33, 34, **62**, 72
cultural minorities 7, 11, 18-21, **19-21**, 37, 40, 43, 57, **72**, **146-7**
cup corals **83**
customs and traditions 11, 32, **33**, 57, **63**, **96**, **125**, **168**

Dagohoy, Francisco 26
Dako Island **141**
dance **7**, **10**, **23**, 24, 32, **32**, 75, **92**, **103**
Dapitan, Mindanao Island 41, **150**
Dauin, Negros Island 93, **112**
Davao, Mindanao Island 35, 40, 135, **142**
deer 14, 15, **171**
deforestation 17, 37, **37**, 41, 115
Dendronephthya sp. **172**
Dinagyang Festival **23**, 24, **92**, 93, **102-3**
Diniwid Beach, Boracay Island **14**, **96**
dipterocarp forests **52**, **78**
diving and snorkelling 18, 38, 39, 40, 41, **48**, **51**, 69, **82**, **84**, **99**, **112**, 115, **120**, **128**, 157, **167**, **168**, **172**
dolphin species 16-17, 40, 93, **113**, **172**
Donsol, South Luzon 16, **90**
drought 17
Dugong 17
Dulang-Dulang, Mount 12, 40, **148**
Dumaguete, Negros Island 93, **110**, **112**
durian **34**, 35

eagles 14, **15**, 17, 18, 37, **77**, 115, 135, **145**, **148**
earthquakes 12, 22, **105**
Easter festivals **1**, 23-4, 38
Echo Valley, North Luzon 57
economic development 28, 29-31, **30-31**, 75, **142**
education 22, 31, 38, 69, **77**, 93
Eland 157, **170**
elections 29, **29**
encomienda system 26, 30
endangered species 17-18, 40, **77**, **90**, 135, **145**, 157, **170**, **171**
endemic species 14, 18
English language 22, **142**
entertainment **7**, **10**, **23**, 24, 32, **32**, 75, **109**, 127, **140**, **151**
environmental problems 17, 31, 38, **76**, **77**, 164
Estrada, Joseph 28, 29
estuarine areas 15-16
Eye-patch Butterflyfish **16**

fauna 14-18, 40, 41
feather stars **83**
festivals and celebrations **1**, **7**, **10**, 19, 23-4, **23**, 35, **64**, **67**, 72-3, **92**, 93, **100-103**, **107**, **134**, **141**, **143**, **152**, **176**

crabs **120**
crafts 34, **47**, **57**, **58**, **117**, **120**, **147**

Filipino people 11, 18-21, **19**, 24
fish farms 17, 38, **38**, **76**, 80
fish species 16, 17, 18, 35, **83**, **99**, **113**
fishing 17, 18, 30, **30**, 31, 41, 43, **44**, **48**, 76, **105**, 113, **115**, **136**, **140**, **151**, **154**, **161**
flooding 13, 17
flora 14-18, 40, **43**, **106**, **108**, **114**, **118**, **135**, **138**
Flower Festival 24
flying foxes 14
folk art **33**, 34
food and drink **4**, **11**, 18, 30, 34-6, **34-5**, 60, 70, **96**
forest areas 13, 14, 15-16, 17, 18, 36-7, **37**, 38, 39, 40, 41, 43, **52**, 57, **58**, 60, 63, 69, **77-8**, **90**, 93, **108-9**, 115, **124**, 135, **140**, **145**, **148-9**, 157, **159**
Fort San Pedro, Cebu Island **119**
Fort Santiago, Manila **26**
forts and watchtowers **26**, **110**, **161**
frangipani trees **118**
Freshwater Crocodile 14, 17, 40
fruit bats 14, 18, 43, **52**
fruit and vegetables **34**, 35, 37, **37**, 39, **62**, 93, **106**, **116**, **152**

games and sports **109**, **127**, **140**, **151** *see also* watersports
General Luna, Siargao Island **141**
geographical survey 11-14, **12-14**, 36-41, **36-41**, 42, 57, 69, 93, 115, 135, 157
geology 12-13 *see also* limestone areas
giraffes 157, **170**
gold and silver 31, **147**
gongs 33
Gorgonian sea fans **16**, **129**
Governor Island 51
government system 27, 28-9, 41
grassland areas 18, **149**
Greater Mouse Deer 15
Green Imperial Pigeon **78**
Green Turtle 16, 17, **18**
Green Wrasse 16
grouper **128**
Guimaras Island 39, 93
Guintubdan, Negros Island **108**, **109**
guitars **119**
Gunter's Cathedral, Coron Island **167**
Guyam Island **141**

Hawksbill Turtle 16
headdresses and hats **21**, **64**, **67**, **92**, **101**
headhunters 21
hermit crabs **120**
herons 17, 40
Hibok-Hibok, Mount 40, **136**, **138**
hiking and walking 17, 18, 40, 43, **55**, 57, **86**, **90**, 93, **144**
Hiligaynon *see* Ilongi dialect
Hill Myna 15
historical survey 11, 18, 20, 24-8, **25**, **27**

INDEX

Homonhon island 25
Hong Kong 27, 31
hornbills 14-15
hot springs 69, **76**, **78**, 93, **106**, **138**, **145**
hotels and guesthouses **47**, **48**, **51**, **52**, **63**, 115, **120**, **156**, 163
houses **26**, **44**, **47**, **67**, **114**, **122-3**, **135**, **135**, **138-9**, **152**, **155**, **160**, **165**, **169**, **172-3**
Humabon, Rajah 22, 25
Humpback Whale 16-17
Hundred Islands **13**, 37, 43, **50**
hunting **129**, **147**

Ibacoy people **57**
Ibaloi people 21, **62**
Ifugao people 21, **21**, 37, **56**, 57, **62**, **64-7**
Iglesia ni Cristo 22
Ilocano dialect 22
Ilocos Norte, North Luzon 29
Ilocos Sur, South Luzon 36
Iloilo, Panay Island **23**, 24, 39, **92**, 93, **102-3**
Iloilo River 39
Ilongo dialect 22
Impala **170**
imported species 41, 157, **170**
Independence Day 28, **28**, **72**
Indonesia 11, 12, 18, 25, 34
industrial development 28, 31, **31**, 43, 115
Intramuros, South Luzon 26, **26**, **71**
invertebrate species 16, **83**, **99**
Iriga, Mount 39
irrigation systems 21, **24**
Isarog, Mount 39
Islam **19**, 21, 22, 23, 25, 28, 32, 33, 34, 36, 41, 135, **152**, **154-5**
islands 11, 12, 36, **37**
  see also individual islands and island groups
Isneg people **62**
Itbayat Island **44**
Ivatan people **20**, 21, 36, 43, **44**

jack fish 16, **128**
Jama Mapun people 21
Java 18, 25
jeepneys **5**, **7**, **33**, 34, **36**, **70**, **89**, **159**
Jolo island group 12
jungle survival techniques **52**

Kabunyian deity figure **62**
Kalagan people **147**
Kalanguya people 21, **62**
Kalibo, Panay Island 24, 93, **100-102**
Kalinga people 21, 57, **62**
Kanlaon, Mount 40, 93, **106**, **108-9**
  Mount Kanlaon National Park **108-9**
Kankaney people **62**
Karaga people 21
Katibawasan Falls, Camiguin Island **138**
the Katipunan 26, 27
Kitanglad mountains 12, 135, **148-9**
Kitanglad Range National Park **148**
Kolibugan people 21
Kulaman people 21
kulintang gongs 33

Labo, Mount 39
Lagen Island **156**
Laguna de Bay, South Luzon

38, **38**, 69, **76**
Lakas Party 29
Lanao Lake, Mindanao Island 21, 40
land ownership/reform 26, 28, 29, 30-31
languages and dialects 11, 18, 19, 21, 22, 33-4, **142**
Lanzones Festival 24
Laoag city, North Luzon 36
Lapu-Lapu (the chief) 25, **120**
La Union, Luzon 36
Legaspi, South Luzon 12, , 38-9, 69, **86-9**
de Legaspi, Miguel 25, 40, **88**, **119**
Leyte Island 12, 29, 40, 115, **130-31**
lianas **78**, **108**
Liguasan Marsh, Mindanao Island 40, 41, **147**
limestone areas 13, **13**, **41**, 43, **50**, **63**, **125**, **132**, 157, **158**, **163**, **168**
Lingayen Gulf **13**, 27, 37, **50**
lionfish **99**, **167**
literature 26, 32, 33-4
logging industry 31
Longhua Temple, Davao **143**
Long-tailed Macaque 14, **132**
Los Baños, South Luzon 69, **77**, **78**
Lucap, North Luzon **50**
Luzon Island 12, 13, 14, 16, 18, **19**, 21, **21**, 22, **24**, 25-6, 31, 36-9, **37-8**, **42-91**, 43, 57, 69
Luzon Strait 36

Mabini, Apolinario 33
macaques 14, 18, 43, **132**
MacArthur, Douglas 27, **27**, **131**
Mactan Island 25, 115, 119, **121**
Mag Asawang waterfall, Negros Island **108**
Magellan, Ferdinand 22, 25, **25**, 115, **121**
Magellan Cross, Cebu City **25**
Maguindanao people 21, 25
Makiling, Mount 38, 69, **77-8**
Malampaya Sound **161**
Malatapay, Negros Island **110**
Malay people 11, 18, **19**, 22, 24, 25, 32, 41, **152**
Malaysia 11, 12, 18, **155**
Mambajao, Camiguin Island **139**
Mambucal, Negros Island 93, **106**
mammal species 14-18, 149, 157
Mamon Island **141**
Mandaya people 21, **147**
mangrove forests 14, 15-16, 17, 18, **52**, **123**, 135, **140**
Mangyan people 21, 25, 39
Manila **7**, 12, 13, 18, 19, 22, 23, 24, 25, **26**, 27, **27**, 28, **28-9**, **33**, 36, 37, **37**, 38, 43, **48**, **68**, 69, **70-71**
Manila Bay 13, 27, 69
the Manila Galleons 26, **84**
Manobo people **20**, 21, 23, **147**
Mansaka people **147**
Manta Ray 18, **129**, 157, **172**
Maranao people 21, 34
Marbel River **144**
Marcos, Ferdinand and Imelda 28, 29, **70**
Marinduque Island 31
marine species 15-17, **16**, 18, **83**, **99**, **112**, 157, **168**
marine turtles 16, 17, 18, **18**, 157, **172**
markets **4**, **11**, **29**, 35, **35**, **71**,

110, **116**, **139**, **152**, **154**
marshes and swamps 13, 14, 17, **20**, 40, 41, **147**
Masbate Island 12, 40, 115
masks **107**, **176**
Masskara Festival **107**, **176**
Matabungkay beach, Central Luzon 38
Mayon, Mount 12-13, **12**, 38-9, 69, **86-9**
the media 22, **142**
medicines 69, 71
Medinilla magnifica **108**
Miagao, Panay Island **105**
migratory birds 18
Mindanao Island 12, 13, 14, 17, 20, **20**, 21, 22, 23, 25, 26, 28, 30, 31, **33**, 40-41, **134-53**, 135
Mindoro island group 12, 18, 21, 25, 27, **38**, 39, 69, **84**
Mines View Park **60**
Miniloc Island 157, **164-5**
mining industry 30, 31
Moalboal, Cebu Island 115, **120**
Molbog people 21
monitor lizards 14
monsoons 13
Moorish Idol 16
Moro Islamic Liberation Front (MILF) 28, 41
Moro National Liberation Front (MNLF) 28
Moslems *see* Islam
mossy forest 18
motorized tricycles **47**, **111**, **120**
mud flats **17**, 18
museums **106**
music and song 32-3, **32**, **75**, **119**

Nakanmuan, Sabtang Island **45**
Nasugbu beach, Central Luzon 38
national parks 17-18, 37, 41, **60**, **78**, **90**, **108-9**, 115, **128**, **131-3**, 135, **140**, **145**, **148**, 157, **172**
  see also wildlife reserves and refuges
National People's Coalition (NPC) 29
Negrito people **19**, 21, 23, 24, 25, 43, **52**, **92**, 93
Negros Island 12, 17, 21, 30, 31, 39, 40, 93, **106-11**
New People's Army (NPA) 28, 40
El Nido Bay, Palawan Island 41, **41**, 157, **162-5**
Northern Sierra Madre Natural Park 18
nudibranchs 16, **83**, **99**

Olango Islands 18
Old Man's Beard **148**
Olive Ridley Turtle 16
Olive-breasted Sunbird **15**
oral traditions 33
orchids **15**, **121**, **135**, **138**, **139**, **143**
otters 15
Oro waterfall, Negros Island **108**
overseas employment 31

paganism 21
Pagsanjan waterfall, South Luzon 69
Palanan Wilderness *see* Northern Sierra Madre Natural Park
Palawan Hornbill 15
Palawan island group **7**, 12, 14, 15, 17, 18, 20, **20**, 21, 22, 24, 41, **41**, **156-73**, 157

Palawan Peacock Pheasant 15, **171**
Pala'wan people 21
Palo, Leyte Island **131**
Pamilacan, Cebu Island **115**, 129
Pampangan dialect 22
Panagsama Beach, Cebu Island **120**
Panay Island **7**, 12, 21, 24, 25, 39, 93, **100-105**
pandanus 148
Pangasinan dialect 22
Panglao Island 40, **126-9**
Pangolin 15
Panhulugan Cave, Samar Island **133**
papaya 35
paraw boats **93**, **95**
parrot species 14
Pasig River 25, 26, **27**, 69, 75
pelagics **112**, **128**, **172**
Pescador Island 115, **120**
pheasant species 15, **171**
Philippine Cockatoo 14
Philippine Crocodile *see* Freshwater Crocodile
Philippine Eagle 14, **15**, 17, 18, 37, 115, **145**, 148
Philippine Eagle Nature Center 135, **145**
Philippine Golden-crowned Flying Fox 14
Philippine Hawk-Eagle **77**
Philippine Independent Church (PIC) 22-3
Philippine Macaque *see* Long-tailed Macaque
Philippine Raptor Center **77**
Philippine Spotted Deer 14
Philippine Tarsier 14, **15**
Philippine White-winged Flying Fox 14
Philippines 2000 programme 28, 31
Philippines University 38, 69, **77**
pigeon species 14, **52**, **78**, **125**
del Pilar, M. H. 33
Pilipino language 22
Pilot Whale 93, **113**
Pinatubo, Mount 12, 13, 28, 37, 38, 43, **54-5**
pine forests 18, 37, **37**, 57, **58**, **60**, **63**
piracy 22, 25, 28, 41, **105**, **110**
political structure 28, 29
Pompadour Green Pigeon **125**
pop art **33**, 34
population density 17, 19, 30, 37, 39, 41, 49, 115, **149**
population migration 11, 18, 19-21, 25, 30, 31, 41, **80**, **149**
ports and harbours 13, 18, 21, 28, 31, **31**, **37**, 38, 39, 40, 43, **52**, **75**, **84**, 150
  see also Manila
pottery 24, **47**, **147**
poverty 17, 19, 28, 30, 31, **122**
power supplies 43, **51**
Puentaspina Orchid Gardens, Mindanao Island **143**
Puerto Galera, Mindoro Island 39, 69, **84**
Puerto Princesa, Palawan Island 41, 157
Pulag, Mount 12, **60**, **62**
  Mount Pulag Natural Park 18
Purple Heron 17, 40
Pygmy Sperm Whale 93

Quezon, Manuel 27
Quezon city, Palawan Island 41

Quezon Island **51**
Quiapo Church, Manila 22, 23, **73**

rainfall 13, 14, 41, **54**
rainforest areas 14, 18, 36-7, 39, 40, 43, **52**, 69, **77**, **90**, 93, **108-9**, 135, **140**, **145**
Ramos, Fidel 28
rattans **78**, **108**
rebellion and insurgency 26-7, 28, 40, 41, 135, **142**
Red Beach, Leyte Island 27, **27**, 115, **131**
Red Jungle Fowl 14
reef fish 16, 17, 18, **83**, **99**, **113**, **128**, **167**, **172**
regionalism 29
religious beliefs 11, 18-19, **19**, 21, 22-3, **22**, **62**, 115, **116**, **118**, **122**, **124**, 135, **143**, **152**, **154-5**
religious relics and artefacts 22, 23, 34, **62**, **100**, **105**, 115, **117**, **130**, **141**
reptile species 14
Ribbon Eel **99**
rice cultivation 21, 24, **24**, 30, 34, 36, 37, 38, **56**, 57, **64-6**, **80**, **88**, 93, **124**, **146**
Rio Grande de Mindanao 13
Risso's Dolphin 16-17
Rizal, José 26, 33, 34, **70**, **150**
Rizal Park and Monument, Manila 26, **27**, **33**, **70**, **72**, **75**
road systems 18, 41, **55**, 57, **68**
rodent species 14
Romblon island group 12, 39, 93
Ropalaea crassa **129**
Roxas, Manuel 28

Sabang, Palawan Island 157, **158-9**
Sabtang Island **44**
Sagada, North Luzon 57, **63**
St Paul's Underground River, Palawan Island 41, 157, **158**
de Salcedo, Juan **47**
Saltwater Crocodile 14
Samal Island 135, **142**
Samal people 21
Samar Island 12, 25, 40, 115, **131-3**
San Fernando, North Luzon 24, 43, **48**, **54**
San Joaquin, Batan Island **44**
San Miguel beer 36
Sangil people 21
sea anemones 16, **83**
sea cucumbers 16, **83**
sea fans **16**, **83**, **129**
sea gypsies 21, **168**
sea squirts **129**
seaweed farms **154-5**, 157, **172-3**
security issues 28
shark species 16, **16**, 18, 39, **90**, **99**, 157, **172**
Short-finned Pilot Whale **113**
Siargao Island 40, 135, **140-41**
Sibuyan Island 18
Sierra Madre Mountains, Luzon 12, 18, 21, 36, 37
Silang, Diego and Gabriela 26
Silliman University 93, **110**, **112**
Sin, Jaime, Cardinal Archbishop of Manila 28
Sinulog Festival 23
Sitangkai, Tawi-Tawi Island 135, **155**
skinks **90**
social structure 19-20

Sohoton National Park 115, **131-3**
soldierfish **83**, **128**
Soleiman, Rajah 25
Sorsogon, South Luzon 39, **90**
Spanish colonial period 11, 18, 21, 22, 23, 24, 25-7, 32, 33, 34, 36, 40, 43, **47**, **71**, **84**, **110**, **117**, **119**, 122, **124**, **161**
Sperm Whale 16-17
spiders **148**
Spinner Dolphin 16-17, 93, **113**
sponges 16, **83**, **99**
star fish 16
stilt and pile houses 135, **155**, 160, **165**, **169**, **172-3**
stinging hydroids **167**
stonefish **167**
Subanon people 21
Subic Bay Freeport 18, 21, 28, 31, **31**, 38, 43, **52**
Subic-Bataan Natural Park 18
sugar cane 30, 36, 39, 40, 93, **106**
Sulu Hornbill 15
Sulu Islands 12, 20, 21, 23, 24, 25, 28, 41, 135, **154-5**
Sulu Sea 15, 17, 18, 41, **157**, **172**

Sumatra 18, 21, 25
sunbirds 15
supernatural beliefs 23
surfing 36, 39, 40, **48**, 135
Surigao, Mindanao Island **140**
sweetlips 16

Taal, Lake and Island 38, 69, **80**
Tabon Cave, Palawan Island 24, 41
Tacloban, Leyte Island 27, 115, **130**
Tagakaolo people 21
Tagalog dialect 22, 33, 34
Tagbanua people **20**, 21, 157
Tagbilaran, Bohol Island 122, **124**
'Taglish' language 34
Taiwan **20**, 21, 24, 36, **44**
Tamaraw 14
Tanon Strait 16-17, 93, **113**
Taoism 22, 23, **40**, **118**
tarsiers 14, **15**
Tasaday people 21
Tausug people 21
Tawi-Tawi island group 12, 36, 135
Taytay, Palawan Island **160-61**
T'boli people 21, 34, 40
temperature range 13, 14
the Ten Datus 25

textiles 21, 31, **33**, 34, **58**, 80, 96 115, **147**
Tingguian people 21
Tondo settlement 25
tourism 17, 18, 34, 37, 39, 40, 43, **50**, **55**, 57, **63**, 69, **90**, 93, **95**, **96**, 115, **120**, 127, 129, 135, **142**, 156, **163**, **164**
trade links 22, 24-5, 26, 34-5, 40, 41, **75**
traditional lifestyles 37, 39, 43, **44**, 57, **67**, **80**, 129
transport and communications **3**, **5**, **7**, 18, **26**, **33**, 34, 36, **36**, 41, 43, **47**, **55**, 57, **58**, **64**, **66**, **75**, **89**, **111**, 115, **120**, 141, 142, 146, 157, **159**
tree corals **172**
tree ferns **108**
tree houses **122-3**
tree species **77**, **118**, **148**
triggerfish 16, **128**
Tubbastrea coral **83**
Tubbataha Reef National Marine Park 18, **18**, 41, 157, **172**
tube worms 16
Tumindao Island **155**
tuna fish 16, **128**, **136**, **172**
Turtle Islands Wildlife Sanctuary 17

turtle species 16, 18, **18**, 157
typhoons and storms 13, 21, **44**, **54**

Vietnam War 28, 38, **52**
Vigan city, North Luzon **26**, 36, 43, **47**
vinta boats **134**, 135, **152-3**
Visayan island group 12, 14, 18, **19**, 21, 25-6, 39-40, **92-133**, 93, 115
Visayan Wrinkled Hornbill 15
volcanoes 12-13, **12**, 28, 37, 38-9, 40, 43, **54-5**, 69, **77-8**, **80**, 86-9, **90**, 93, **106**, 108-9, 135, **136**, **144**

wage levels 30
Wallace Line 15
Waray-Waray dialect 22
water buffalo **124**
water supplies **51**, **60**, **88**
waterbuck **170**
waterfalls 69, **88**, **108**, **138**
watersports 18, 36, 38, 39, 40, 41, **48**, **51**, 69, **82**, **84**, **99**, **112**, 115, **120**, **128**, 135, 157, **167**, **168**, **172**
Whale Shark 16, 39, **90**, **129**
whale species 16-17, 40, 93, **113**, **129**, **172**
White Beach, Boracay Island **6**, **39**, 93, **93**, **95**, **96**

Whitetip Reef Shark 16, **16**
wild pig 14, 43
wildlife 14-18, **15-16**, 18
wildlife reserves and refuges 13, 17-18, **17**, 37, 41, **50**, 93, 135, **147**, 157, **167**, **170-71**
see also national parks
women **10**, **19**, 20, 31, **32**, **58**, **139**, **141**, **143**, **147**
woodcarving 34, **62**
World Bank Conservation of Priority Protected Areas Project (CPPAP) **148**
World War II (1939-45) 27, **27**, 28, 115, **119**, **131**, 157, **167**
World Wide Fund for Nature (WWF) **129**
wrasses 16
wreck exploration 157, **167**

Yakan people **19**, 21, **33**, **154**
Yapak Beach, Boracay Island **95**, **96**

Zambales Mountains 12, 13, 37
Zamboanga city, Mindanao Island 41, 135, **152**
Zamboanga peninsula, Mindanao Island 41, **134**
zebra 157, **170**

PHOTOGRAPHIC ACKNOWLEDGEMENTS

The publishers extend their thanks to the following people who kindly loaned their photographs for inclusion in this book. With the exception of those listed below, the photographs in this book were taken by **Nigel Hicks**.

J. Allan Cash Ltd: pages 58 (below left and bottom right), and 86 (top left and right))

F. Jack Jackson: pages 16 (all three subjects), 18, 19 (bottom centre and bottom right), 30 (right), 33 (below left), 34 (left), 84 (middle left), 98 (above right and below), 99 (middle right), 112 (above left), 113 (right), 129 (top), 152 (above and top), 154 (above left and left), 155 (below right), 166 (below left), 167 (right), 169, 172 (right)

Michael Freeman: pages 22, 119 (below), 152 (far right), 154 (above right)

Maurice Joseph: pages 56, 64 (above left), 66 (below right and above left), 67 (right)

Norma Joseph: pages 1, 21, 31 (below), 35 (below), 64 (above right and far right), 66 (above right), 67 (above)

Philippines Department of Tourism: pages 107 (all three subjects), 147 (both subjects), 176

Photobank: page 10

Diana Salevourakis: pages 70 (below left and below right), 135, 138 (bottom), 139 (bottom), 150 (above and left), 151 (right, below, and bottom)

Jon Spaull: pages 32 (below right), 57, 71 (below right), 146 (both subjects)

Travel Ink/Abbie Enock: page 134

Life File/Jon Woodhouse: page 80 (above left)